Brain Science for Lawyers, Judges, and Policymakers

Brain Science for Lawyers, Judges, and Policymakers

Owen D. Jones
Glenn M. Weaver, M.D. and Mary Ellen Weaver Chair in Law, Brain, and Behavior
Professor of Law
Professor of Biological Sciences
Vanderbilt University
Director, MacArthur Foundation Research Network on Law and Neuroscience
Director, Weaver Family Program on Law, Brain Sciences, and Behavior

Jeffrey D. Schall
Professor of Biology
Canada Research Chair in Translating Neuroscience
Director, Visual Neurophysiology Centre
York University
Member, MacArthur Foundation Law and Neuroscience Project

Francis X. Shen
Professor, University of Minnesota Law School
Teaching Faculty Member, Center for Bioethics, Harvard Medical School
Member, MacArthur Foundation Research Network on Law and Neuroscience
Chief Innovation Officer, Massachusetts General Hospital Center for Law, Brain and Behavior

Morris B. Hoffman
District Judge (ret.), Second Judicial District (Denver), State of Colorado
Member, MacArthur Foundation Research Network on Law and Neuroscience
Research Fellow, Gruter Institute for Law and Behavioral Research

Anthony D. Wagner
Lucie Stern Professor in the Social Sciences
Department of Psychology and Wu Tsai Neurosciences Institute
Stanford University
Member, MacArthur Foundation Research Network on Law and Neuroscience

OXFORD
UNIVERSITY PRESS

OXFORD
UNIVERSITY PRESS

Oxford University Press is a department of the University of Oxford. It furthers the University's objective of excellence in research, scholarship, and education by publishing worldwide. Oxford is a registered trade mark of Oxford University Press in the UK and certain other countries.

Published in the United States of America by Oxford University Press
198 Madison Avenue, New York, NY 10016, United States of America.

Library of Congress Cataloging-in-Publication Data
Names: Jones, Owen D., author.
Title: Brain science for lawyers, judges, and policymakers / Owen D. Jones,
Jeffrey D. Schall, Francis X. Shen, Morris B. Hoffman, Anthony D. Wagner.
Description: New York : Oxford University Press, 2024. | Includes index.
Identifiers: LCCN 2023043413 (print) | LCCN 2023043414 (ebook) |
ISBN 9780197748862 (paperback) | ISBN 9780197748855 (hardback) |
ISBN 9780197748886 (epub) | ISBN 9780197748879 | ISBN 9780197748893
Subjects: LCSH: Practice of law—Psychological aspects. |
Law—Psychological aspects. | Neurosciences.
Classification: LCC K346 .J659 2024 (print) | LCC K346 (ebook) |
DDC 612.8/23302434—dc23/eng/20231005
LC record available at https://lccn.loc.gov/2023043413
LC ebook record available at https://lccn.loc.gov/2023043414

DOI: 10.1093/oso/9780197748855.001.0001

Note to Readers

This publication is designed to provide accurate and authoritative information in regard to the subject matter covered. It is based upon sources believed to be accurate and reliable and is intended to be current as of the time it was written. It is sold with the understanding that the publisher is not engaged in rendering legal, accounting, or other professional services. If legal advice or other expert assistance is required, the services of a competent professional person should be sought. Also, to confirm that the information has not been affected or changed by recent developments, traditional legal research techniques should be used, including checking primary sources where appropriate.

(Based on the Declaration of Principles jointly adopted by a Committee of the American Bar Association and a Committee of Publishers and Associations.)

ODJ: To Kelty
JDS: To Michelle
FXS: To Simone and Gabriel
MBH: To Kate, and to Margaret Gruter
ADW: To Naomi and Kieran

CONTENTS

ACKNOWLEDGMENTS

This book would not have been possible without the generous support, for which we are most grateful, of the John D. and Catherine T. MacArthur Foundation, the MacArthur Foundation Research Network on Law and Neuroscience, the Weaver Family Program on Law, Brain Sciences, and Behavior, and our scholarly homes: Vanderbilt University, York University, University of Minnesota, and Stanford University.

We also thank Martha Farah, Kelty Jones, Read Montague, Marc Raichle, Alara Weitkamp, Hendrik Weitkamp, and anonymous peer reviewers for providing very valuable input and feedback on earlier portions—and sometimes full drafts—of this manuscript.

We benefited from the sharp eyes and work of a number of research assistants, including Faheem Ali, Farah Arif, Sarah E. Bourgeois, Joseph B. Hendricks, Jamie Stewart, Sonia Subramaniam, and Rachel Wagner. Thanks, too, to the entire Shen Neurolaw Lab.

We thank Alexandra Trelle and Subbulakshmi S for substantially assisting with a number of the MRI-based brain images.

Quenna Stewart, as always, provided terrific administrative support.

LIST OF FIGURES

FOREWORD

There are many books introducing brain science to non-scientists, but this book is unique among them. Its aim is to cover the fundamentals of neuroscience that are most relevant for lawyers, judges, policymakers, and those interested in the extent to which rapid advances in our understanding of how the brain works might affect legal doctrine, policy, and practice. Law, after all, concerns the regulation of human behaviors, and those behaviors come from human brains. Although we focus here on U.S. law, many efforts across the world are being undertaken to apply the insights of neuroscience to legal problems.

Thanks largely to some amazing technological developments, we have learned more about how the human brain works in the last thirty-five years than we learned in all of prior human history. But because of the almost unimaginable complexity of the brain—not just the number of brain cells but also their dense connections and complicated ways of communicating—we are just beginning to peer into the still largely opaque black box that is the brain.

The clarity of what we can currently see depends greatly on the level of organization at which we are looking. We know quite a lot about brains at the microscopic level, how individual brain cells work and how they communicate with one another. We also know a fair amount about how brains are organized into large interconnected functional regions. For example, we know quite a lot about the regions containing the visual pathways of the brain, through which we apprehend selected slices of the world around us, knowledge highly pertinent to legal issues such as the reliability of eyewitness testimony. We know less about the *prefrontal cortex,* a region necessary for higher-order cognitive functions like foreseeing consequences, deciding what to do, and withholding undesirable actions, functions pertinent both to wrongdoing and the judgment of wrongdoing, as well as a person's competence and ability to make reasoned decisions.

But our understanding at what we might call the circuit level of organization—how brain cells organize into circuits, and circuits organize into larger networks across regions—is still rudimentary. Neuroscientists are beginning to understand some building blocks of brain circuitry, but they are far from explaining how groups of just thousands of the 86 billion neurons in the average human brain form parallel, serial, and recursive circuits, and networks of circuits across different brain regions to actually accomplish the operations necessary for seeing, foreseeing, deciding, and acting. As a result, we know very little about how brains make decisions, how they form intentions, or how they turn those intentions into actions—exactly the kinds of complex questions that the law regularly asks.

Moreover, individual brains vary widely based on genetics, development, and experience. As the science now stands, there is often too much variation between individual brains to be able to reach reliable conclusions about how a particular brain functioned in the past, is functioning now, or will function in the future, if we were to base that conclusion solely on what we know about the average brain. But of course in applying the law, we are almost always concerned with a particular individual, not groups of individuals. Was *this defendant's* brain too diseased to form an intent to kill? Was *this decedent's* brain too compromised for him to have testamentary capacity? Is *this* plaintiff's brain hurt so badly that she will never be able to work again?

Given that neuroscience remains a young field, and given the complicated kinds of individual questions typically posed by the law, why do legal consumers need a primer on neuroscience? The answer is that at virtually every point in the legal system—legislative, regulatory, civil, and criminal litigation—policymakers, lawyers and judges are already beginning to encounter or use neuroscience, whether it's ready for prime time or not. Legislators are relying on brain science to craft new laws; regulators are relying on it to promulgate rules and adopt regulations; lawyers are using it to decide whether to file cases and, after filing, whether to settle or plea-bargain them; and even Supreme Court justices are sometimes referencing brain development when they draw lines like how old murderers must be before they can be constitutionally sentenced to life without the possibility of parole.

The use of neuroscience to answer legal questions is not just happening, it is accelerating. As neuroscience is used in more and more legal contexts, policymakers, lawyers, and judges need a working framework of scientific knowledge in order to decide whether the neuroscience really has anything to add. Such a framework is needed to address questions like these: Is increased activity in certain brain areas really an objective indication of chronic pain? Can lying be detected reliably by functional brain imaging? Is taxpayer money better spent researching the neuroscience of alcoholism or the neuroscience of PTSD? Are psychopaths—who regularly show demonstrably different brain activities in regions associated with moral judgment—incapable of being rehabilitated? Ready or not, these questions are here, and the legal community needs to know enough about neuroscience to be able to decide whether it can help answer any of them.

Given that neuroscience cannot currently answer most legal questions, one might ask why legal actors need to bother at all with its details. Why doesn't this primer consist of one sentence: "Not yet ready." There are several answers.

First, it has been our experience that legal actors—and, really, most lay consumers of science—tend to overstate, not understate, the lessons of an emerging science. Learning the basics of neuroscience, the capabilities and limits of various brain measurement methods, and the challenges of inferring mental states from brain processes will teach legal players *why* much of the science is not generally ready for widespread legal use, despite the lure that it should be.

Second, there are some narrow but important legal issues on which neuroscience may currently have something important to add—for example, neuroimaging studies may inform some clinical diagnoses, such as antisocial personality disorder, depression, and CTE (chronic traumatic encephalopathy—the condition that can be caused by football collisions).

Third, just thinking about traditional legal questions in nontraditional ways, and in particular in neuroscientific ways, may give us productive new legal perspectives. For example, do the four traditional legal mental states in criminal law reflect real and psychologically distinct brain states, and might those brain states be impacted differently by various intoxicants?

Finally, and maybe most importantly, neuroscientific advances are happening rapidly. Some legal issues that neuroscience cannot answer today may be answerable by the time this book reaches a particular reader in the not-too-distant future, as neuroscientists around the world accelerate the pace of their discoveries.

That pace is hard to overstate. The ability to measure human brain function without entering the skull was invented in the 1980s, and today neuroscientists can not only make those measurements with increasing exactness, they can even influence the decisions of an experimental participant. Functional brain imaging gained common use in the 1990s, and today neuroscientists can partially decode perception, recognition, memory, and intention from brain-imaging signals. The ability to sample signals from dozens or hundreds of individual neurons was achieved in the 2000s, and today neuroscientists can use such signals to allow quadriplegics to control robot arms.

The future trajectory of these technological advances remains steep. To name just one of several examples, the National Institutes of Health is funding an ambitious program called the Brain Research through Advancing Innovative Neurotechnologies (BRAIN) Initiative, which aims to foster widespread innovation and novel neurotechnologies. Tomorrow, some of these new BRAIN technologies will almost certainly find their way into the legal system. Legal consumers will have to know the neuroscience basics before they will be able to determine whether these new technologies will be able to shed new light on any particular legal question.

This book has ten chapters. Chapter 1 samples the kinds of legal questions neuroscience is already being asked to answer, and Chapter 2 presents an overview of the human brain.

Chapter 3 begins our two-chapter look at brain structure, starting at the gross (nonmicroscopic) level of the organization of the cerebral cortex, the outer layer of the human brain. Chapter 4 extends this exploration by examining the collections of neuronal structures located inside the brain, beneath the cortex. Chapter 5 shifts from brain structure to brain function by looking at neurons—what they are and how they work.

The next two chapters cover the basics of brain imaging: Chapter 6 examines the imaging technologies that reveal brain structures; and Chapter 7 examines the imaging technologies that reveal brain functions. The imaging technologies reviewed in these two chapters include x-ray, computed axial tomography (CAT or just CT), electroencephalography (EEG), magnetoencephalography (MEG), positron emission tomography (PET), single-photon emission computed tomography (SPECT), and magnetic resonance imaging (MRI), as well as a form of MRI that measures the degree of connectedness between different parts of the brain, known as diffusion tensor imaging (DTI).

Chapter 8 examines technologies that can change brain function, including deep brain stimulation (DBS), by which electrodes surgically implanted in the brain can relieve some disorders such as Parkinson's disease, and two technologies used primarily for research, by which parts of the brain close to the skull can be activated or deactivated temporarily: transcranial magnetic stimulation (TMS) and transcranial direct current stimulation (tDCS).

Chapter 9 discusses the limits and cautions of all these technologies, including their spatial and temporal limitations, the assumptions embedded in the collection and analyses of the brain data, and the statistical and logical cautions that accompany any effort to claim that designated brain areas or defects in those areas "cause" or even coincide with certain behaviors. Chapter 10 muses about the kinds of legal questions neuroscience technologies might be able to help answer in the future.

Throughout, we keep things short because we believe brevity will be most useful for our legal consumers. The book is intended to be short enough to be read easily cover to cover, but comprehensive enough to be useful as a reference tool for particular neuroscience issues that may arise in legal contexts. Readers who want to dig deeper can do so by consulting the material listed in the Further Readings and Resources section at the end of the book. We also provide a large glossary of scientific and neuroscientific terms, which we italicize when we first discuss them in the text, and a comprehensive index.

A final note on what this book is not. It is not a legal primer, but rather a neuroscience primer. We will therefore not cover any legal issues in any depth, including those related to the admissibility of neuroscientific evidence. But of course, understanding the neuroscience should inform, and is intended to inform, the inquiry into whether a particular kind of neuroscientific evidence is sufficiently reliable and probative for its intended legal purpose, whether its prejudicial impact outweighs its probative value, and thus whether it should be admitted as evidence in a hearing or trial. We discuss some of these legal issues very generally in the penultimate chapter, but the details of that inquiry are beyond the scope of this science primer. Readers interested in deeper aspects of this intersection of law and neuroscience are encouraged to consult the Further Readings and Resources section at the end of the text, and in particular the coursebook that three of us wrote: O. Jones, J. Schall, & F. Shen, Law and Neuroscience (2nd ed., Aspen Coursebook Series, Aspen Publishing, 2021).

To remind readers why a basic understanding of neuroscience is important to legal consumers, we begin each chapter with the summary of a real legal controversy in which neuroscience played some role. These vignettes are not necessarily tied to the subject matter of the chapter they introduce, but are instead intended to give readers a flavor of how neuroscience is being used in actual legal controversies. We have organized them roughly from what we think was the most responsible use of neuroscience (well-established medical diagnoses) to the least responsible (lie detection by EEG).

We've aimed to keep grounded in the basic science, because we want our legal readers to learn the basic science. We recognize that every conversation about the brain tends to lure participants, scientists and non-scientists alike, into speculating about Big Questions, including the natures of free will, right and wrong, individual responsibility, and (increasingly in this era of advancing robotics and artificial intelligence) humanity itself. These are questions that also preoccupy many legal philosophers. But we have intentionally stayed away from them. District attorneys trying to figure out whether a defendant's brain scan justifies a more lenient plea offer, or Social Security officials trying to decide whether a citizen's traumatic brain injury is permanent, don't need theoretical tracts on moral philosophy or artificial intelligence; they need answers about the present state of brain science.

We thank the John D. and Catherine T. MacArthur Foundation and the Weaver Family Program on Law, Brain Sciences, and Behavior for their generous financial and institutional support. Each of us had the privilege of being associated with the MacArthur Foundation's Law and Neuroscience Project and/or its successor, the MacArthur Foundation Research Network on Law and Neuroscience. We also thank the Gruter Institute for Law and Behavioral Research. This book would not have been possible without the rich interdisciplinary culture that these associations fostered.

Owen D. Jones, Nashville
Jeffrey D. Schall, Toronto
Francis X. Shen, Minneapolis
Morris B. Hoffman, Denver
Anthony D. Wagner, Palo Alto

1

WHERE WE ARE NOW

"An individual who has sustained either (1) irreversible cessation of circulatory and respiratory functions, or (2) irreversible cessation of all functions of the entire brain, including the brainstem, is dead. A determination of death must be made in accordance with accepted medical standards."

Uniform Determination of Death Act (UDDA) (1981)
(adopted in some form in all 50 states).

"Should the term 'irreversible' be replaced by the term "permanent"? and "How should objections to the use of neurologic criteria to declare death be handled?"

Questions posed by the Uniform Law Commission to a drafting committee formed in 2022 to recommend updates to the UDDA.

INTRODUCTION

Before we dive into the brain science, let's sample some of the areas of law already being impacted by neuroscience. This is by no means a comprehensive analysis. It is meant only as a survey, to give readers a sense of today's overlap between law and neuroscience.

We have organized our survey into the three traditional legal categories of civil, criminal, and administrative law, and within those categories we focus on three domains: case law, legislation, and regulation. We recognize there are many other legal actors operating at the intersection of law and neuroscience, but because legislation and regulation are officially recorded, and many court decisions reported, we focus our survey on these three domains because there is actual data about them. Indeed, an important part of the scholarly work being done today at the intersection of law and neuroscience is the systematic and comprehensive measurement of the extent to which neuroscience is appearing in legislative, regulatory, and court records.

Brain Science for Lawyers, Judges, and Policymakers. Owen D. Jones, Jeffrey D. Schall, Francis X. Shen, Morris B. Hoffman and Anthony D. Wagner, Oxford University Press. © Oxford University Press 2024.
DOI: 10.1093/oso/9780197748855.003.0001

But we do not forget, and ask readers not to forget, the cast of legal actors standing behind formally reported legal actions: lobbyists and other citizens using neuroscience to try to convince legislators to pass laws or regulators to regulate; lawyers using neuroscience to advise their clients and to explain to them legal positions taken, not taken, or taken then abandoned; lawyers using neuroscience to negotiate settlements with other lawyers before disputes go to trial and sometimes even before they make it into court; and even voters expressing their views on legal issues that might be informed by neuroscience.

There is one more group of legal actors we will only mention here: law professors. A growing number of law schools now offer classes on law and neuroscience, sometimes called "neurolaw," and indeed several of the authors of this book have taught such classes. Legal scholars, sometimes working with neuroscientists, are also producing a large literature about the intersection of law and neuroscience. We anticipate that all of these academic developments will have a substantial impact on the practice of law, and it is to the practice of law that we now turn.

By one admittedly limited measure—the use or attempted use of neuroscience as evidence in the courtroom in reported cases—forensic neuroscience is exploding. From its first use in the early 1900s—in cases involving primitive lie detection using measurements of blood pressure and respiration rates—the frequency of neuroscientific evidence in court has grown dramatically, not just in the United States but in many other countries, including Canada, the Netherlands, England, and Wales. To give some perspective on this growth, the cumulative number of reported U.S. cases involving electroencephalography (EEG) evidence—just one of many kinds of neuroscientific evidence—grew from 8 in the decade of the 1940s, to 204 in the 1960s, 344 in the 1980s, 576 in the 2010s, and already to 1,367 in just the first three years of the 2020s.

This growth in forensic neuroscience was both quantitative and qualitative, in the sense that it didn't take long after the invention of new neuroscience technologies, primarily imaging technologies, to find their way into courtrooms. One of the reasons for this rapid evidentiary absorption was the U.S. Supreme Court's landmark 1993 decision in *Daubert v. Merrell Dow Pharmaceuticals, Inc.*, which was decided before most of these new techniques were invented, and which arguably increased the likelihood new neuroscience techniques would be accepted into evidence despite their novelty. This growth in the courtroom use of neuroscience has been paralleled in the legislative and regulatory realms, though at a somewhat less robust rate.

One last but important point about sampling the use of neuroscience across legal domains: our sampling is meant to be value-neutral, in the sense that we are describing the ways in which policymakers and lawyers are *trying* to make use of neuroscience to advance their positions, and judges and juries to resolve disputes. We do not mean to suggest that the neuroscience is always, or even often, making a difference. No doubt much of the legislation and regulation we mention would have been enacted without its neuroscience gloss. Likewise, in many of the court cases represented in our sample, maybe most of them, the neuroscience might not have mattered; indeed, in many of those cases judges refused to admit it into evidence. It is difficult, if not impossible, to measure with any confidence the impact that neuroscience evidence is having in reported cases, though a substantial amount of anecdotal evidence suggests it has mattered in many cases.

CIVIL LAW

We divide our survey of the use of neuroscience in civil law into the areas of torts, contracts, constitutional law, health law, family law, and probate.

Torts

Because the law of torts is the law of civil damages for negligently and intentionally caused injury, it should come as no surprise that neuroscience has had its deepest and broadest civil impacts in torts. All manner of imaging techniques, from x-rays to functional MRI, have been used to try to show that a plaintiff has or has not suffered structural and/or functional brain injuries as a result of defendants' actions. In the latter category of functional loss, these imaging techniques are typically coupled with traditional psychological or neuropsychological examinations. Neuroscience has also been used to attempt to show the likelihood of future impairment, an important component of tort damages. Another important component is pain—past and future. Especially in the category of chronic pain, which we discuss in Chapter 10, neuroscience has been used generally to explain the phenomenon, although at the moment chronic pain cannot be reliably diagnosed by neuroimaging.

Cases that involve the claims of negligently or intentionally caused traumatic brain injury (TBI) now regularly include structural MRI images as part of psychological or neuropsychogical evaluations, both on the plaintiff and defense sides. Claims of more subtle and difficult-to-diagnose conditions—such as mild cognitive impairment from low-impact automobile collisions or sports-related concussions—are increasingly using functional MRI in clinical neuropsychological evaluations, again on both sides of the courtroom. Product liability cases alleging brain damage (for example, from defective seatbelts) now routinely use neuroimaging to help prove or disprove the damage. Similarly, malpractice cases involving imageable brain conditions, and of course those claiming the negligent interpretation of those images, rely heavily on brain imaging.

In addition to common law torts, there is also the litany of private causes of action implied or expressed in various kinds of legislation, including prohibitions against discrimination, consumer fraud, and invasion of privacy, that are mirroring their common law cousins in terms of the use of neuroscientific evidence, primarily to prove or disprove damages.

Legislation and regulations having tort impacts have been adopted in Congress and across many states, covering tort-related topics as varied as autism, post-traumatic stress disorder (PTSD), addiction, and TBI from sporting activities. These statutes, rules, and regulations address these areas in a host of different ways, from establishing funds for victims suffering from these conditions, to funding education and research, to extending or tolling statutes of limitations.

Contracts

Neuroscience, again usually paired with traditional clinical observations and testing, has been used in breach of contract cases where contractual capacity is raised as an issue, both to contest and defend capacity. Similarly, neuroscience has been used to support and defend against claims of contractual duress.

In a narrow range of breach cases, tort-like damages may be recoverable in some jurisdictions, and in those cases neuroscience has been brought to bear on these kinds of damages. It has also been used in bad faith cases brought against insurance companies when they fail to cover brain-related claims. Another area at the boundary of tort and contract is fraud, and neuroscience had been used by and against defendants claiming that a brain condition prevented them from forming the intent necessary to defraud, including debtors in bankruptcy cases claiming that diminished cognitive function prevented them from intentionally defrauding creditors or the court.

Constitutional Law

Neuroscience has made legislative, regulatory, and courtroom appearances in several different types of noncriminal constitutional contexts, including efforts by video game makers to enjoin on First Amendment grounds state legislation prohibiting the sale of violent or sexually explicit video games to minors, and by litigants and policymakers to address various kinds of abortion issues, including the hotly contested issue of when in their development fetuses can feel pain (as exemplified by the quotations from the *Dobbs* amici briefs that begin Chapter 8). In Section 1981 civil rights litigation, where plaintiffs have asserted claims of brain-related injuries, neuroscience evidence has been used in all the ways it has been used in ordinary tort cases. Neuroscience has even played a constitutional role in immigration, with immigrants arguing that their removal would violate the Eighth Amendment's ban against cruel and unusual punishment because they would be institutionalized in their home countries due to their mental conditions.

Health Law

Neuroscience evidence has been used in a variety of health law disputes and policies. Whether it is prisoners claiming prison officials are failing to treat their brain diseases or conditions, civilly-committed citizens arguing they are no longer dangerous to themselves or to others, insureds disputing an insurance company's decision not to cover brain-related claims, parents claiming school officials have failed to tailor required individual educational plans to their children's brain diseases or conditions, or regulators and legislators addressing each of these listed issues, neuroscience has played an increasingly prominent role.

One especially fertile legislative area has been the mandating of health insurance coverage for certain diseases, including autism, PTSD, and other mental diseases and disorders. Neuroscience has also been relied on by legislatures creating and funding a vast array of programs addressing things like substance abuse, mental health, and early childhood intervention and education.

Family Law

Neuroimaging has been used in custody disputes to show one spouse suffers from some condition interfering with the ability to parent (including TBI, early onset Alzheimer's disease, and even claimed proclivities to violence) and in property division and support contexts to show a spouse or child is in need of expensive medical treatment. In dependency and neglect proceedings aimed at terminating parental rights, neuroimaging has been presented to prove or disprove the state's claim that a parent's debilitating brain condition rendered him or her unfit.

Probate

Probate controversies almost always revolve around the mental state of the legal target of the proceedings, whether testator, settlor of a trust, or person-to-be-protected, and neuroscience evidence has been used in all of these kinds of proceedings. It has been used in will and irrevocable trust contests to bolster or rebut claims of duress and lack of testamentary capacity, as well as in guardianship and conservatorship proceedings aimed at the mental capacity of the person to be protected (as in the case example that begins Chapter 2). It has also been used in care and treatment cases, typically class actions, in which chronically mentally ill claimants assert that the state and its agencies have failed to comply with statutory treatment mandates.

CRIMINAL LAW

Neuroscience evidence is now commonly used to supplement traditional clinical testimony supporting or attacking a defendant's competence to stand trial, a juvenile defendant's request to be tried as a juvenile rather than as an adult, and the reliability of eyewitness identification, of the testimony of child victims, and of confessions. At trial, neuroscience evidence is now commonly used to help bolster or defeat claims of insanity or the inability to form the required state of mind.

Indeed, the use of neuroscience by the defense in these contexts, both pretrial and trial, is now so common, especially in high-stakes cases like first degree murder, that the failure of defense counsel to use it has now become a common postconviction ground for claiming defense counsel was ineffective.

Neuroscience is playing an increasingly prominent role in sentencing, where the rules of evidence are typically relaxed, and an especially important role in capital sentencing, where juries are required to decide whether to impose the death penalty, and in so-called *Miller* hearings, where judges must decide whether juvenile murderers sentenced to life without the possibility of parole should be given parole dates. When neuroscience is used at these sentencing trials or hearings, it is typically used to bolster or rebut claims that the defendant has some kind of mitigating brain condition, such as severe schizoaffective disorder or antisocial personality disorder or was especially brain-immature. However, lawyers and academics have raised the possibility that some of these mental conditions might in fact be viewed as aggravating rather than mitigating (a phenomenon the literature calls "the double-edged sword"), especially by jurors and judges concerned about a defendant's future dangerousness.

Appellate courts have relied on neuroscience to draw difficult constitutional lines in criminal cases, including the age at which criminals may be held responsible, the age juvenile defendants may be tried as adults, and how old juvenile murderers must be before they face the death penalty or life without the possibility of parole.

Even at the final stages of the criminal process—probation, incarceration, and parole—neuroscience is making its presence felt. It has been used by probation departments, especially in sex assault cases or with defendants who have prior convictions for sex assault—to help courts and prison officials craft appropriate treatment conditions. Courts and prison officials have used it to help them determine whether defendants should be classified as "sexually violent predators," a classification that in many jurisdictions has direct impacts on prison placement and treatment. Neuroscience has been used by parole boards to decide whether prisoners should be released early.

Legislatures and regulators have been active in using neuroscience to step into virtually every aspect of the criminal justice system not occupied exclusively by the courts. They have relied on neuroscience to create specialty courts, including drug courts and mental health courts, to create and alter victims assistance programs, to require courts to admit neuroimaging evidence in competence hearings, to change the punishment of sex offenders, to limit the circumstances juveniles can be tried as adults or sentenced to life without parole, to change probation and parole rules and processes, and even to define the "shaken baby syndrome."

ADMINISTRATIVE LAW

Great swaths of administrative law are adjudicative, and neuroscience is touching those swaths in the same way it is touching adjudication in courts. Thus, litigants in Social Security cases are using brain scans to bolster or defend against claims of disability based on brain conditions, such as epilepsy. Medicare and Medicaid disputants likewise sometimes use neuroimaging to support or refute claims and to appeal or resist the appeal of denied claims. Workers' compensation claims—mirroring tort claims that would have been brought in court but for the exclusivity of administrative remedies—have also seen neuroscience being offered to show or disprove brain-related injuries or conditions.

Neuroscience is also being used to help justify a dizzying variety of rules and regulations touching almost every imaginable aspect of our lives, from the licensing of child-care facilities (the neuroscience of early childhood development) to regulating the kinds of medications that can be dispensed at opioid treatment clinics (see the example that begins Chapter 3), and everything in between. Lobbyists and lawyers trying to achieve or avoid a regulatory result, and regulators trying to accommodate different policy perspectives, have all used neuroscience to make their regulatory arguments and decisions.

***

So, what do lawyers, judges, and policymakers need to know about neuroscience as they face it in all these different legal situations? We begin to answer that question in the next chapter.

2

OVERVIEW OF THE BRAIN

Thirty-seven-year-old Mary Ezenwa met 87-year-old Alan Carlin on a website called millionairematch.com, proclaimed her love for him in their second email, and married him one month later. Alan's son Peter brought a guardianship and conservatorship proceeding, claiming that his father suffered from a condition called cerebral amyloid angiopathy—a buildup of amyloid protein in the brain's blood vessels, which can cause hemorrhaging and progressive strokes. Peter claimed his father had suffered from progressive strokes, causing significant deficits in "areas of the brain responsible for frontal lobe functioning", limiting his father's judgment and insight and leaving him personally and financially vulnerable. Peter's lawyer presented medical evidence of this condition along with recent past examples of Alan losing tens of thousands of dollars to various scammers. Mary had not stolen anything from him, but she did tell him (falsely) that she was worth $5 million, and she gained access to a bank account he opened when they moved in together. The probate court not only entered the requested guardianship and conservatorship orders, it also issued a permanent restraining order against Mary, preventing her from having any contact with Alan. Mary appealed the restraining order, and it was affirmed.

In re Carlin, 16 Wash. App.2d 1057 (2021).

INTRODUCTION

You already know more about the brain than you think. You know that the brain and not some other organ (like the heart, as was once believed) is the source of thoughts, emotions, and decision-making. You also know your brain is located inside your skull, has a top and bottom, and a surface and interior.

You probably have heard that the brain has an outer mantle called the cortex, and that the cortex has different parts, or lobes, that have been associated with different

Brain Science for Lawyers, Judges, and Policymakers. Owen D. Jones, Jeffrey D. Schall, Francis X. Shen, Morris B. Hoffman and Anthony D. Wagner, Oxford University Press.
DOI: 10.1093/oso/9780197748855.003.0002

functions like perception, movement, thought, and emotion. You've probably also heard that your brain has two sides, or hemispheres, and that the right hemisphere handles sensations from and movements in the left side of the body, and the left hemisphere sensations and movements from and in the right side of the body. You may know that your brain works through specific chemical and electrical processes, that the brain cells that implement those processes are called "neurons" and that brains are built from a very large number of neurons (roughly 86,000,000,000 in the average human adult).

That's a good start. All we need to do now is to fill in some details, particularly those that may be helpful for understanding and applying brain science in legal settings. This chapter focuses on getting you oriented to the basic architecture of the brain. Later chapters will build on this foundational knowledge, providing more information on structure and function.

We begin this chapter with a few cautionary notes about what's known and not known about how the human brain works. We then discuss the brain's place in the nervous system, its gross (that is nonmicroscopic, or macroscopic) anatomy and the critical role the circulatory system plays in getting brains the energy they need. We finish the chapter with a discussion of terminology that describes locations in and on the brain.

PROCEED WITH CAUTION

Throughout this book, we try to strike an appropriate balance between the truly remarkable things now known about the brain and the vast, still-unknown territory. As in so many other domains of knowledge, people tend to be either overly enthusiastic or overly skeptical. We strive to be neither. And we encourage the same approach by readers.

For instance, we should be enthusiastic about the fact that clinicians and scientists today can identify many kinds of brain damage in living people without cutting open their heads. That's a pretty remarkable clinical achievement. Yet we should be skeptical about how easy it may be to infer, with suitable precision, what the legal consequences of that brain damage might be. The implications of technological breakthroughs are rarely obvious. And that's particularly true when we are talking about the complex kinds of intentions, memories, emotions, pains, and behaviors the law usually cares about. It is one thing to be able to see a tumor growing in an individual's brain, and quite another to say what the tumor has to do with the individual's ability to enter into contracts, form intentions, or resist temptation.

At the outset, you should be aware that the brain's functions are only partially localized. For example, the rear of the brain is mostly involved in interpreting stimuli from the eyes to enable vision. The front of the brain is involved in making plans and decisions. But you should keep in mind that a single brain region contributes to multiple functions, and a single function requires multiple brain regions. Moreover, different brains look and function differently. Just as two commuters might arrive at the same place using different routes, two brains might accomplish the same task by recruiting different brain networks.

Given these complexities of brain function, one should be wary when reading popular press accounts about the discovery of "centers" in the brain such as the "love center" or the "music center." While it's true that brain function is in part localized, neuroscientists today increasingly talk about "circuits" and "networks" rather than "centers." Because the brain is so richly interconnected and because any given region typically does a number of different things—often depending on which other regions are simultaneously active and interacting with it—it is a gross oversimplification to say that one part of the brain is solely devoted to one function.

Moreover, the language we use to describe a part of the brain can itself add confusion or introduce errors. For example, the law will often encounter descriptions of brain regions (e.g., "prefrontal cortex") that are too broad because they encompass multiple regions (ventrolateral, dorsolateral, and frontopolar prefrontal cortices) associated with different functions. This complexity of the brain and of the mappings from structure-to-function can create challenges for determining which level of description is relevant for any given legal issue and thus what evidence from neuroscience is germane.

Let's consider the *insula*, a structure you will learn about later, as an example of this problem of mapping brain structure to brain function. The insula, tucked away deep in the cortex, is involved in the experience of disgust, an important emotion favored by evolutionary processes because it helps organisms avoid food that can sicken or kill. Just think back to the last time you had food poisoning, and to the food that caused it. Your stomach is probably churning now at the mere thought. That's disgust, and it's being animated in part by your insula.

The insula is also involved in assessing blame, which can be regarded as a kind of social disgust, and which was also important evolutionarily as our small tightly knit groups struggled with the problem of when and how to punish norm violators. Today, this phenomenon of social disgust remains an important legal consideration when, for example, judges decide on criminal punishment or jurors decide whether a civil defendant has acted merely negligently or with reckless disregard.

But the insula is also involved in many other functions having nothing to do with physical or social disgust. These include the regulation of blood pressure, the ability to sense where parts of our body are in relation to each other, the recruitment of effort to perform complex tasks, the perception of pain, laughing, crying, and even empathy. Such a jack-of-all-trades can hardly be called the "disgust center," any more than it can be called the "blood pressure center." We will see this heterogeneity of function in nearly every brain region and circuit we discuss.

The fact that brain circuits that evolved to signal disgust at dietary dangers can also signal disgust about social dangers illustrates one of the brain's most interesting characteristics. Namely, structures that evolved in the service of one function gained the capacity, over long periods of evolutionary time, to contribute to many other tasks. The insula also nicely illustrates our point that the way we describe brain locations can be ambiguous. Depending on the descriptive level, the "insula" contains between two and thirteen separate parts. The parts are distinguished by their internal structure and by the connections they have with other parts of the brain. Those different internal structures and their external connections enable different functions.

Finally, while neuroscientists use the shorthand *insula* as if this were a distinct physical structure of the brain that could be unplugged from the whole, that's not how brains are built. Neither the insula nor any other area of the brain we will be discussing is like a discrete circuit board snapped into place. Rather, the brain is a dense network of cellular connections, more like a jungle ecosystem than a machine built of parts. The function of a given region at any moment in time depends, in part, on the states of the other brain regions with which it is interacting at that moment in time.

The brain is a beautiful, stunning, complex collection of circuits. The central problem in understanding how these circuits work is that most of them are doing something at all times. That makes it very difficult to trace the path of cause and effect through the brain. If that were not enough, the neurons in the brain are almost unimaginably interconnected. You may remember a diagram of a nerve cell from high school, showing a few input connections and one or two outputs. But the average neuron in the human cortex has between 1,000 and 10,000 connections! Ferreting out which specific set of neurons is doing what work is extremely hard, and modern brain-imaging methods, despite their advances, cannot alone answer the question of causation.

Scientists have investigated the brain's organization from two complementary perspectives—macroscopic and microscopic. We will see in later chapters that brain imaging and other technologies have given us a good understanding of the location of large brain regions, when they are activated, and how activation varies across brain regions in or out of concert. Likewise, as we will see in Chapter 5, an enormous amount is known about how individual neurons synthesize inputs and communicate with each other. Still, very little is known about the brain's intermediate level of organization, that is, how groups of neurons form networks and networks of networks. It is at this intermediate level of organization that much of the brain's work gets done, especially the higher order things the law cares about—controlling impulses, forming intentions, and making decisions.

For legal consumers of neuroscience, the long and short of this puzzle about matching brain structure and brain function is that if you are ever faced with experts who claim some legal relevance because a party's "empathy center" or "responsibility center" or other legally relevant "center" is impaired, know that those experts are either grossly oversimplifying the neuroscience, or don't know what they are talking about.

THE BRAIN'S PLACE IN THE NERVOUS SYSTEM

Anatomists typically divide the human body (following the plan of all animals with spinal cords) into a handful of main systems. One is the nervous system, which is composed of the brain, the spinal cord, and all the nerves emanating from the brain or spinal cord. *Nerves* are bundles of the communication cables—called *axons*—through which specialized cells—called *neurons*—influence muscles, glands and other neurons. This is easiest to remember by noting that "axon" and "away" both begin with "a." Nerves carry electro-chemical messages between the brain and other parts of the body and within the nervous system.

Some nerves are one-way streets—carrying messages only *to* the brain *from* the senses of the body (these are called afferent nerves) or only *from* the brain *to* muscles and glands (efferent nerves). Other nerves are two-way streets that contain both afferent and efferent pathways. Examples of afferent nerves—sending a message from the body to the brain—include the sensory nerves from your eyes that enable you to read this text. Examples of efferent nerves—sending a message from the brain to the body—are the nerves to the muscles in your arms and hands that allow you to turn a page or move a cursor.

Other than the nerves to and from the face and head, called *cranial nerves*, all the others pass between the brain and spinal cord through the *brainstem*. The brainstem is a collection of structures that sits below the brain and atop the spinal cord. Because it is the gate through which virtually all nerves pass and because it houses nerve circuits supporting vital body functions, damage to the brainstem can affect everything from heart rate and breathing to sleep cycles and consciousness. Consequently, the brainstem plays an important part in the debates about brain death, and injury to the brainstem can the basis of civil lawsuits.

Noncranial nerves exit the brainstem and enter the spinal cord to then emerge at different levels of the spine before they extend out into the body. Neuroscientists call this extension of nerves into the body *enervation*. The fact that nerves emerging from different levels of the spinal cord enervate different parts of the body explains why injuries to different levels of the spinal cord cause paralysis in different parts of the body.

The nervous system consists of two major parts: the *central nervous system* (CNS), consisting of the brain and the spinal cord (and a few of the cranial nerves); and the *peripheral nervous system* (PNS), consisting of the nerves that project to (afferent) or emanate from (efferent) the spinal cord and enervate the body (plus the remaining cranial nerves not considered part of the CNS) (Figure 2.1). Whether afferent or efferent, central or peripheral, the *cell bodies* of most neurons are in the brain, which receives all the incoming signals and sends all the outgoing signals.

The nervous system is connected to, and integrates the functions of, all the other body systems. Because the brain is connected to every other part of the nervous system, it is thus ultimately connected to every other part of the body. It receives sensory inputs from both the outside world (through smell, taste, touch, hearing, and sight) and the inside world (e.g., from your limbs and your guts).

The outside sensory messages include signals from nerves in the skin, visual messages from the optic nerves, sounds from auditory nerves, smells from olfactory nerves, and tastes from nerves in the tongue. The inside messages include messages about body temperature, heart and respiration rates, stomach distention, time of day, sleepiness, and the state of glandular excretions from the endocrine system. The brain integrates these incoming sensory messages into an *autonomic* "state of the body" assessment. The purpose of all this monitoring, combined with information already active in the brain (such as current states of thought and emotion), is to enable the brain to choose what to do next. Sometimes this choosing is through conscious deliberation, as when we choose an item from a menu. But most of the time it's more automatic, as when we breathe, sneeze, blink, or walk. Sometimes it may be arguably something in between, as when we angrily pull the trigger on a gun.

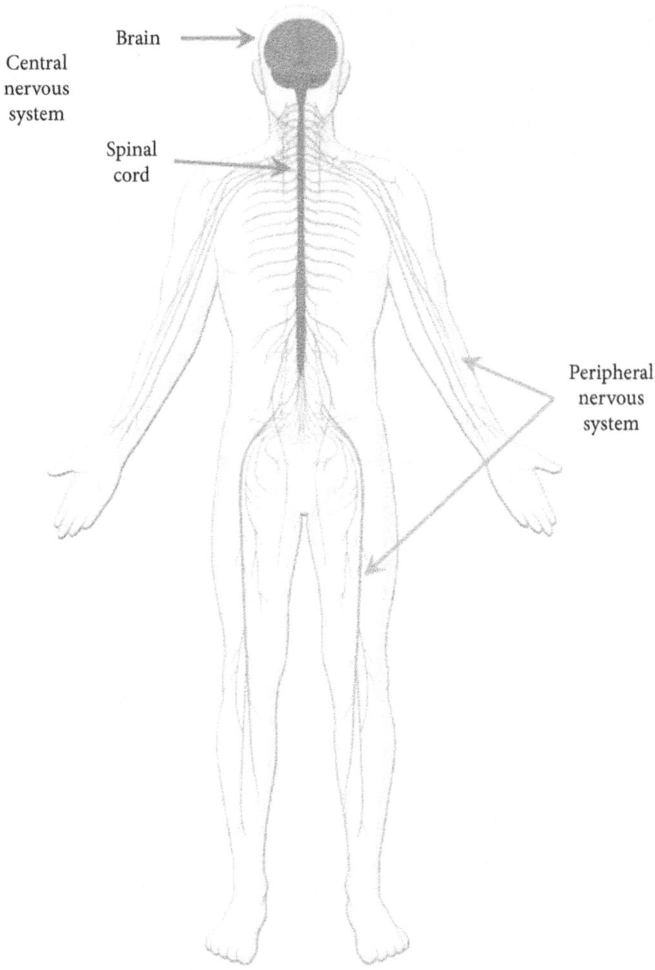

FIGURE 2.1 Central and peripheral nervous systems.

Modern neuroscientists have called the brain the world's most sophisticated prediction machine. Roughly speaking, it takes in data about the body and the body's environs, combines it with existing brain states, and makes a prediction about what will happen next and what it should do to optimize its own survival based on what will happen next. If the prediction is that the rock falling down the side of the mountain will hit your car if you don't take evasive action, then you take evasive action.

BRAIN ANATOMY: THE BIG PICTURE

The brain sits in the skull, beneath a set of nurturing and protective structures known as the *meninges*, which include the *dura*, *arachnoid mater*, and *pia mater*. The dura (from the same root as the word "durable") is a thick membrane between the skull bones and the arachnoid mater (named for its spider-web character), with the pia mater ("delicate material") coating the brain. Cerebrospinal fluid circulates between the arachnoid mater and pia mater.

Some anatomists divide the brain into three large parts: (1) the *cerebrum* (Latin for "brain," and what most people probably picture when they think of the brain); (2) the brainstem; and (3) the *cerebellum* (Latin for "little brain," a large structure below and behind the cerebrum, perched upon the brainstem) (Figure 2.2). The brainstem, as we have seen, is important because it is the structure through many of the nerves between brain and body pass, and includes circuits that keep the heart breathing and lungs inflating. The cerebellum is involved prominently in the timing and coordination of movements like walking and balance, and also makes contributions to motor learning (like swinging a golf club) and aspects of higher-level cognition such as language, *working memory* (the ability to keep information in mind), and *executive function* (which supports goal-directed thought and behavior).

The entire cerebrum, both surface and interior, is comprised of two similarly shaped but distinctly folded *hemispheres*—the right and left hemispheres, labeled from the viewpoint of the brain's owner—that are strongly interconnected (predominantly through a structure called the *corpus collosum*). Although almost all the structures and functions of both the interior and surface are mirrored in each hemisphere, the match is not identical. Some important functions (particularly those associated with language) depend more heavily on structures in one of the two hemispheres. Neuroscientists are still trying to work out the relationship between the two hemispheres.

Pop psychological claims that high order functions are broadly lateralized between the right side (creativity) and left side (logic) and that creative people are that way because their right hemisphere is more active have largely been debunked. Almost everything the brain does, especially higher order functions, are distributed widely across the two hemispheres, and nearly all functions in the healthy brain ultimately emerge from the integration of information across the hemispheres.

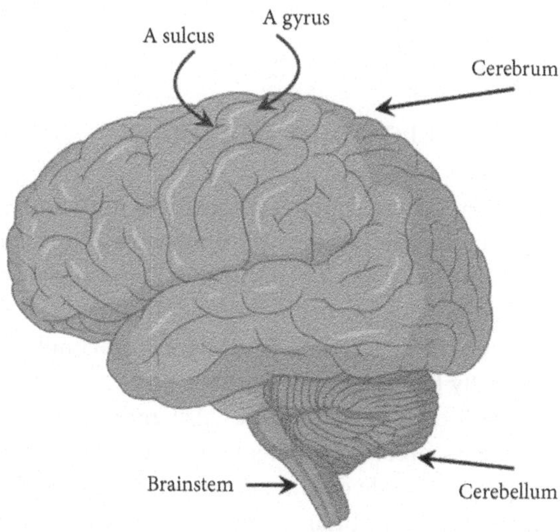

FIGURE 2.2 Cerebrum, cerebellum, and brainstem (also showing a sulcus and gyrus).

The *cortex*, short for "cerebral cortex," is the wrinkly outermost mantle of the human brain. There are actually multiple types of cortex, some evolutionarily older than others. The human brain is notable for having a strong predominance of the evolutionarily newest type of cortex termed, aptly, *neocortex*. Given that about 90% of human cerebral cortex is neocortex, as a shortcut scientists often refer to that outermost mantle simply as the cortex. We will adopt that convention here. When we say "cortex" we mean the neocortex. Sometimes parts of the cortex are indicated by using the word "cortex"—such as "primary motor cortex"—and this convention means this is an area that is a part of the cortex, not a stand-alone cortex, of which there is only one in each hemisphere.

The word cortex comes from the Latin word for "bark," as in the bark or outer mantle of a tree. The wrinkling of the cortex, which is present in almost all large-brained mammals, allows a larger surface area to be squeezed into a small volume. If the adult human cortex were removed and flattened out, it would be the size of a large pizza. It is comparatively thin, averaging the thickness of a doctor's tongue depressor. But the folds are deep; more than two-thirds of the surface of the human cortex is hidden in the folds. Each fold creates valleys, which neuroscientists call *sulci* (pronounced "sul-sigh," singular *sulcus*, pronounced "sul-kus") and hills, which they call *gyri* ("jai-rai," singular *gyrus*, "jai-russ") (Figure 2.2).

We will be spending a lot of text describing the structures and functions of the cortex because it is crucial for the kinds of higher order activities the law cares about. There are many discrete areas and structures within the cortex, and we will be discussing several of them and their functions in the next chapter.

There are likewise many structures below the cortex, filling the interior of the brain. The function of some of these interior structures will be covered in Chapter 4. They are important because they interact with the cortex to enable all that the brain does, including perception of and movement in the world, risk and reward processing, motivational, emotional, and attentional integration, awareness of others and of ourselves, and many forms of learning and memory for events, facts, habits, and skills.

BLOOD IN THE BRAIN

The way the circulatory system supplies oxygen and nutrient-rich blood to the brain is important to understanding how the brain works, how scientists measure brain function, and how blockages or ruptures of blood vessels can damage the brain. As we will see in Chapter 6, the relationship between blood flow and brain function is central to how several brain-imaging technologies work. Those technologies can't really be understood without understanding how blood gets to the brain and what it does once it's there. Also, many different brain diseases are diseases of the brain's circulatory system. One of the most common is occlusion, or the blockage of a blood vessel that can sometimes result in its explosion and resultant hemorrhage, in the brain. Such *cerebral vascular accidents* are known commonly as strokes.

It should be evident by now that the brain does a lot of work. From writing that brief or contract to regulating your blood sugar to producing the latest bizarre dream, the brain works around the clock. Like most body parts, the brain does not create its own energy; it must have energy delivered to it. Like all organs of the body, the brain's power source is oxygen and glucose delivered by the blood.

The brain is the body's biggest energy hog. On average, it comprises only about 1/40 of an adult human's total body mass, yet commands 1/5 of the body's total oxygen supply. The brain contains a few hundred miles of blood vessels; that's why head wounds can bleed so much. That number may seem impossible, until you consider that every one of the brain's 86,000,000,000 neurons must be supplied with blood, typically by submicroscopic-sized capillaries.

The human brain's blood supply starts with two sets of large arteries—the two carotid arteries, one on each side of the neck toward the front, and the two vertebral arteries, one on each side of the neck toward the back. Pairs of arteries running off these main arteries communicate across the brain's midline and supply the front and back of the brain. Another set of arteries connects the two hemispheres. These arteries link in a circuit that balances blood pressure within the brain. Critically, this circuit also provides an alternative path for the blood to flow to both hemispheres if a major supply to one hemisphere becomes blocked. (It takes some time for this alternative circulatory pathway to get engaged, which is why even some small blockages in one hemisphere can cause stroke.)

Neuron function and blood supply are closely related. To understand how, we need to introduce a second type of brain cell, called the *glia*, which is Greek for "glue." Glial cells form a superstructure to support the proper development and healthy function of neurons. In addition to supporting the neurons structurally, scientists are discovering that glial cells play an important role in critical brain functions, including helping to regulate the supply of blood to neurons. Neurons can send signals to a type of glia known as *astrocytes*, calling for more or less blood. This neural/glial circulatory feedback circuit is the basis for the astonishing imaging technologies we will explain in later chapters. Those technologies work not by measuring brain activity directly but rather by measuring the circulatory effects of that activity. So, for example, PET scans can be used to measure the amount of radioactively tagged blood in a brain area—the inference being that more blood is called for by regions doing more metabolic work.

Like all energy-consuming parts of the body, when brains consume oxygen and glucose they release metabolic byproducts that need to be removed. The deoxygenated blood also needs to get recycled back to the heart and lungs to get re-oxygenated. To accomplish these tasks, the brain has a kind of drainage system, composed of large empty areas near the surface called *sinuses*. Some of the metabolic waste products and used blood collects in the sinuses. Other waste and used blood deeper in the brain are removed by tiny veins. Larger veins then remove the waste and used blood from both of these systems. Those veins combine into the main large veins draining the brain—which you know as the jugular veins (one on each side).

This drainage feature of the brain's circulatory system is the foundation for many of the *biomarkers* that are being explored for brain injuries such as traumatic brain injury and diseases such as Alzheimer's. Traumatic injury and disease may alter brain cells in such a way that certain proteins find their way into the blood exiting the brain. This might one day allow clinicians to better diagnose—from a simple blood draw—whether an individual has a concussion or a particular brain disease; indeed, it is now possible to measure the levels of key proteins associated with Alzheimer's in blood plasma. These blood-based diagnostic methods would have clear legal implications if a particular diagnosis was an issue in a legal dispute.

Precisely because the brain needs so much blood, it is vulnerable to small compromises to its blood supply. A tiny clot, which is typically harmless in other organs, can cause stroke and death if it gets stuck in the brain. The brain's need for oxygen can be compromised in other ways, including high altitudes and surgery.

The brain is also susceptible to a host of chemicals that are disruptive or even toxic. To guard against such insults, mammalian brains are equipped with a *blood-brain barrier*. This barrier is not a single physical barricade, but instead is an architectural feature of the brain's circulatory design: the brain's blood vessels get smaller and smaller as they approach the neurons they supply, dividing into submicroscopic capillaries with diameters just a little larger than a red blood cell (approximately 10 micrometers, or 10 millionths of a meter). One reason these submicroscopic capillaries are so small is because they must be so plentiful. Researchers believe that every neuron in the brain is supplied by its own submicroscopic capillary. An additional benefit of this small size is that these submicroscopic capillaries block anything larger than the average red blood cell from reaching neurons—this is what is meant by the blood-brain barrier.

The protective advantage of the blood-brain barrier can be a disadvantage when it comes to treating some brain disorders. Many drugs developed to help with diseases or other debilitating processes in the brain cannot be ingested orally or injected into the bloodstream, because they get blocked by the blood-brain barrier and never reach their targets in the brain. Clever pharmacological manipulations can sometimes help.

For example, you may have heard of a drug called L-DOPA, short for levo-dihydroxyphenylalanine, which is used to treat Parkinson's disease among other things. Parkinson's disease is caused principally by a shortage of dopamine, which we will see in Chapter 5 is an important neurotransmitter that allows signals to pass from neuron to neuron. But patients with Parkinson's disease can't simply be injected with additional dopamine because the dopamine molecule will not pass through the blood-brain barrier. However, L-DOPA, which is a metabolic precursor of dopamine, will pass through the blood-brain barrier, whereupon it is converted into dopamine.

HOW TO DESCRIBE BRAIN LOCATIONS

We now discuss the words scientists use to describe directions and identify locations on and in the brain. This language of location is critically important not just to brain researchers but also to legal consumers of brain science. As we have already seen, the term "prefrontal cortex" sweeps in a number of smaller regions involved in different but overlapping functions. Damage to one of these smaller regions could have substantially different functional impacts than damage to others, depending on the behavior and situation. In order to distinguish between the smaller parts of larger regions, and even just to locate the larger regions inside the head, scientists have developed a specific language of brain geography.

Like surveyors and mapmakers, researchers and physicians have agreed on conventions about how to describe brain locations. Unfortunately, different scientific disciplines tend to use different conventions. Adding to the confusion, the conventions have changed over time, and some older conventions persist together with the new. Even within a single research paper, several different locating systems might be used.

A moment's thought will convince you that locating parts of the brain is a little more challenging than locating points on the globe, which requires only an agreement about lines of latitude and longitude. Two numbers are enough to specify a location on the surface of the Earth, but to describe locations inside the brain, we will need to use a third dimension. In addition, the brain is of course not a sphere, human brains vary between individuals, and even a single individual's brain grows in size and changes shape over time.

Neuroscientists cannot use directions like east, west, north, and south. But they do use directions like up, down, front, back, side, middle, right, and left. Because of anatomy's roots in Greek and Latin, neuroscientists tend to use directional words from the history of medicine, like anterior for front and posterior for rear. Some of the medical words have synonyms, and some neuroscientists alternate between directional synonyms pretty freely. Here's a list of the most common of these medical directional words, with their synonyms and ordinary meanings:

Medical directional words, synonyms	Ordinary meaning
anterior, rostral	toward front
posterior, caudal	toward back
dorsal, superior	toward top
ventral, inferior, basal	toward bottom
lateral	toward side
medial	toward middle

These terms are commonly used in all of physiology and medicine, not just neuroscience. Thus, the famous "ACL" of football injury fame is the *anterior* cruciate ligament, a knee ligament closer to the anterior or *front* of the knee.

We teach our students a few tricks to remember these directional terms. Anterior must mean front, because it is the opposite of posterior, and we all know what posterior means. Rostral, a synonym for anterior or front that actually means "nose," is related to the word "rostrum"—the lectern at the *front* of the room used by speakers. If you forget what "dorsal" means, maybe you can remember that the dorsal fins of a fish are on top. "Basal," of course, is related to the word base, or bottom. You'll probably just have to memorize "caudal," or you can remember that it means "tail." These three sets of locational terms are used to describe directions in the brain (Figure 2.3).

The cerebral cortex, of special interest to legal consumers because it contains regions critical to complex brain functioning, consists of more than 200 structurally and functionally distinct areas identified by various classification schemes. One of those schemes depends on the fact that different neurons from different areas of the cerebral cortex vary in cellular structure and density, which can be seen when one stains brain tissue and examines it under a microscope. These variations were first comprehensively noted in the early 1900s by a German anatomist named Korbian Brodmann. He described the variations systematically, working from the top (dorsal) part of the brain to the bottom (ventral). Brodmann distinguished fifty-two areas of the human brain based on the appearance and arrangement of the neurons found in them and labeled the areas numerically. Neuroscientists and clinicians today still often refer to the Brodmann area ("BA") numbers. So, for example, BA4 is the motor strip, or primary motor cortex, which enables movement. It is number 4 just because Brodmann distinguished the first three areas in the posterior adjoining part of the cerebral cortex.

As neuroscientists learned more about the cerebral cortex and new tools became available—such as the ability to use MRI to measure brain function and connectivity—they realized that Brodmann's description was incomplete and in places inaccurate. By drawing on cellular structure and density, along with data about function and connectivity, scientists now believe that there are three to four times more distinct brain areas than Brodmann identified. Nevertheless, Brodmann

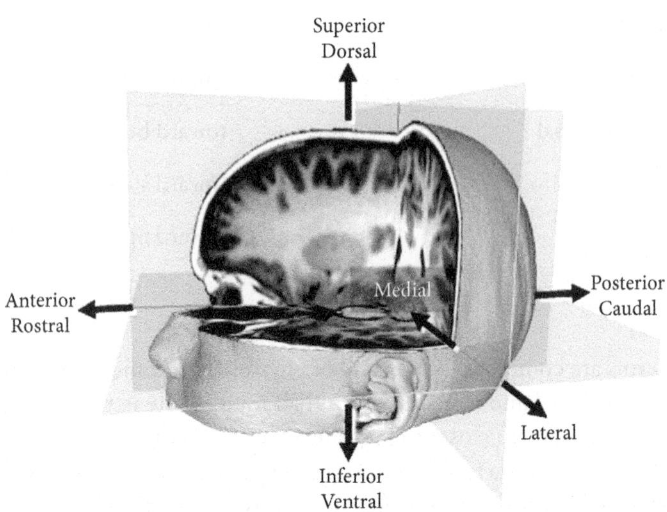

FIGURE 2.3 Terms used for directions in the brain and head.

areas are still used by physicians and medical researchers, and that's why anyone discussing brain geography needs to be fluent with them.

To overcome the inadequacies of the Brodmann system, neuroscientists developed agreed-to systems of coordinates that attempt to account for individual brain differences and differences in age and development. The first of these systems, named after one of the French neurosurgeons who developed it, is called the Talairach system. It was based largely on postmortem analysis of one hemisphere from a single brain of a sixty-year-old female. A newer coordinate system, based on the aligning and averaging of MRI scans from 152 individuals, was developed by the Montreal Neurological Institute (MNI), and it is called the MNI coordinate system. Whether one adopts the Talairach or the MNI coordinate system, their application to a subject brain requires alignment of that brain to the coordinate system, which can be achieved with some precision—in part, because relative distances between different brain structures are fairly similar across people. But these coordinate systems will always have some error—because each person's brain differs in small and sometimes large ways from the average.

Neuroscientists may occasionally refer to Brodmann areas (for areas in the cortex) or to the Talairach coordinate system, but since the advent and widespread adoption of MRI methods, research papers often adopt the MNI coordinate system when describing a specific location in the brain—such as where increased activity was observed during functional brain imaging or where brain stimulation was applied.

But it is also common for neuroscientists to use descriptive systems that locate places in the human brain just by describing where those places are in relation to other well-known regions or structures. These methods are akin to ordinary street addresses, versus the latitude/longitude approach of coordinate systems like MNI. The address 123 Main Street, Anytown, Delaware, USA, is a method of describing a location that does not depend on longitude and latitude but rather on labels we have given to large areas, like Anytown, Delaware, and USA. Instead of Talairach or MNI coordinates, most brain descriptions use these kinds of labeled directions.

These directional labels are often used together to better pinpoint an area. In that case, the convention is to write them so the location can be discovered by reading the address right to left, just like we do with ordinary street addresses: 123 Main Street, Anytown, Delaware, USA requires us first to locate the USA, then Delaware, then Anytown, then Main Street, then 123.

Let's try an example. A famous area of the brain in neuroscientific circles, which we will be discussing in Chapter 3, is the dorsolateral prefrontal cortex (or dorsolateral PFC), abbreviated DLPFC. Reading from right to left, we start at the cortex ("C"), or outer layer of the brain, so we know this is on or near the brain surface and not in the interior; then we move to the front part of that cortex ("F"); then we move to the *very* front (pre) part of it ("P"); then we move to the side (lateral) of that prefrontal cortex ("L"); and finally we move to the top (dorso, meaning dorsal) of that lateral prefrontal cortex ("D"). The DLPFC in one hemisphere (the RIGHT) is shown in Figure 2.4.

Sulci and gyri (remember, valleys and hills) can also be used as locational markers, at least for locations in the cortex. Thus, for example, the lateral sulcus is the obvious

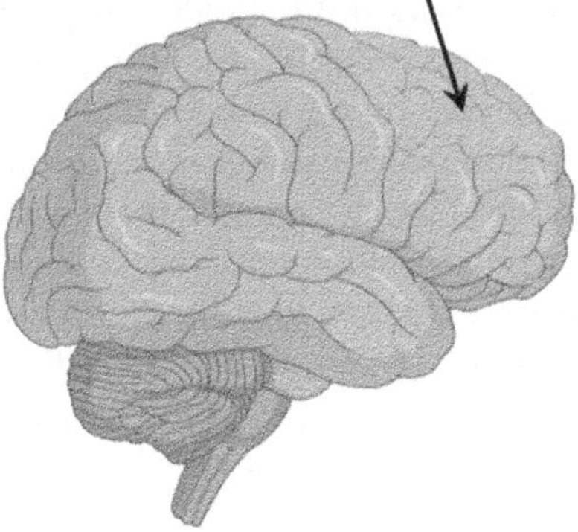

FIGURE 2.4 Right dorsolateral prefrontal cortex.

gap dividing the temporal lobe below from the frontal and parietal lobes above. The *central sulcus,* or *central fissure,* is another prominent sulci on the cortex, running down each side of the cortex from the center top (dorsal medial). The central sulcus separates the frontal from the parietal lobe.

Neuroscientists also use three perpendicular axes, akin to the Talairach or MNI coordinates, but they use them not to locate brain areas using coordinates but rather to describe the orientation of the two-dimensional cuts their neuroimages represent, and then to describe locations within those cuts. These three mutually perpendicular axes are oriented just the way you would expect: one going front to back (anterior-posterior), one going up and down (dorsal-ventral), and one going side to side (medial-lateral). The three axes are named by their directions: (1) the anterior-posterior axis; (2) the dorsal-ventral axis; and (3) the medial-lateral axis.

These three lines not only orient us directionally, they also define three mutually perpendicular planes. As we will see in Chapters 6 and 7, several imaging technologies take computerized slices of measurements through the brain, and neuroscientists use the names of these three defined planes to describe the orientation of the imaging slices: *horizontal* (sometimes *axial*), *coronal,* and *sagittal* (Figure 2.5). These three names can be a little confusing; one helpful hint is that they don't describe the location of the observer but rather the location of the cut.

Thus, the horizontal plane (also known as the *axial* plane) is a horizontal cut through the head, such as one made a bit above the ears, dividing the brain into a top portion and a bottom portion. All neuroimages taken parallel to this horizontal plane are called horizontal images. Horizontal images give the perspective of one looking down onto the top of the subject's brain. Particular locations within a horizontal slice are described as being toward the front versus back (anterior/rostral versus posterior/caudal) and toward the center versus outside (medial versus lateral). The medial-lateral descriptions are also sometimes supplemented with a right versus left description (though this can be confusing; more about that in a moment).

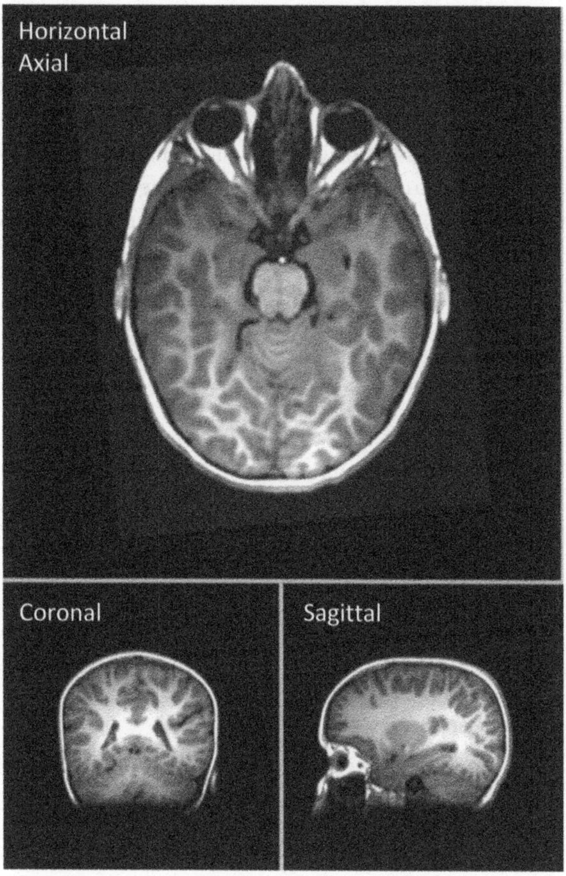

FIGURE 2.5 The three standard orientations of brain imaging.

The coronal plane is a vertical slice, such as one passing just in front of our two ears and dividing the brain into a front portion and a back portion. Coronal images are taken from the perspective of looking at the front of the person's face, and locations on coronal slices are described as being toward the top versus bottom (dorsal/superior versus ventral/inferior/basal) and toward the center versus outside (medial versus lateral) and sometimes right or left.

Finally, the sagittal plane is a vertical slice that cuts along the longest axis of the brain, such as the plane that cuts the nose into two halves and the brain into its two hemispheres. "Sagittal" comes from the Latin word for arrow, so you can think of the sagittal cut as a bunch of vertically stacked arrows coming right at the face and slicing the head into two sides. Sagittal images of the brain look from the side of the person, and locations on sagittal slices are described as being toward the front versus back (anterior/rostral versus posterior/caudal) and toward the top versus bottom (dorsal versus ventral/basal). By the way, you may get confused looking at sagittal slices about which is the front of the brain and which is the back. An easy trick is to find the "overhang" and think of it as a baseball cap. That's the front of the brain, where the forehead, eyes, and nose are.

A caution about the descriptors "right" and "left" when it comes to describing brain locations in horizontal and coronal slices. Radiologists and other physicians have a long tradition of reversing the left/right directions on their horizontal and coronal images, so that when they are facing patients and talking to them the orientation of the patient matches the orientation of the image the doctor is looking at. Thus, if you have a broken rib on your right side, the image the doctor is looking at will show it on the doctor's left side, but that will match your right side. Neuroscientists no longer follow this medical convention. When modern neuroscience papers refer to left and right, they typically mean from the person's point of view.

Now that we know how to describe locations on and in the brain, let's begin our tour of the brain from outside in, starting in the next chapter with a survey of the outermost layer, the cerebral cortex.

3

THE CEREBRAL CORTEX

Opioid dependence and some of the most distressing opioid withdrawal symptoms stem from changes in another important brain system [in addition to the mesocorticolimbic network—the so-called risk-reward network], involving an area at the base of the brain—the locus ceruleus (LC). Neurons in the LC produce a chemical, noradrenaline (NA), and distribute it to other parts of the brain where it stimulates wakefulness, breathing, blood pressure, and general alertness, among other functions. When opioid molecules link to [naturally occurring opioid receptors called] mu receptors on brain cells in the LC, they suppress the neurons' release of NA, resulting in drowsiness, slowed respiration, low blood pressure—familiar effects of opioid intoxication. With repeated exposure to opioids, however, the LC neurons adjust by increasing their level of activity. Now, when opioids are present, their suppressive impact is offset by this heightened activity, with the result that roughly normal amounts of NA are released and the patient feels more or less normal. When opioids are not present to suppress the LC brain cells' enhanced activity, however, the neurons release excessive amounts of NA, triggering jitters, anxiety, muscle cramps, and diarrhea.

T.R. Kosten & T.P. George, "The Neurobiology of Opioid Dependence: Implications for Treatment," 1(1) Sci. Pract. Perspect. (July 2002): 13–27.

[T]hese regulations establish the procedures by which the Secretary of HHS determines whether a program is qualified to dispense opioid agonist medications in the treatment of opioid use disorders [including methadone, levoalpha-acetylmethadol (LAAM) and naltrexone], and standards regarding the appropriate quantities of opioid agonist medications that may be provided for unsupervised use by individuals undergoing such treatment.

Medications for the Treatment of Opioid Misuse Disorders, Proposed Rule by the United States Department of Health and Human Services, December 16, 2022.

Brain Science for Lawyers, Judges, and Policymakers. Owen D. Jones, Jeffrey D. Schall, Francis X. Shen, Morris B. Hoffman and Anthony D. Wagner, Oxford University Press.
DOI: 10.1093/oso/9780197748855.003.0003

INTRODUCTION

To begin our tour of the cerebral cortex, we must introduce some details about its key constituent, the neuron. Neurons come in many sizes and shapes, the variation in form corresponding precisely to variation in function. In spite of this variability, scientists recognize three key parts of each neuron, which we introduce here because these different parts are responsible for the different ways early anatomists described the cortex. Essentially, every neuron has three parts: (1) *cell body*, or *soma*; (2) *axon*; and (3) *dendrites* (Figure 3.1).

The cell body, or soma, is the part of the neuron that contains the cell's nucleus. The nucleus houses the neuron's genes and other machinery to keep the cell alive.

The axon is the fiber leading from the neuron's cell body, along which an "output" signal from that neuron may be communicated to downstream neurons (or to muscles or glands). Each neuron has one axon emerging from its cell body, but that axon can connect to thousands of other neurons. Axons can span short distances, within the cerebral cortex, for example. They can also span long distances, up to three feet, from the spinal cord all the way to the most remote part of a limb.

The dendrite is the "input" portion through which the neuron receives the signals or influences from other neurons. Unlike the single axon, multiple dendrites branch off the cell body, and their further branching can resemble trees and bushes. Each of these dendritic branches can receive thousands of signals from the axons of other neurons. We will explain in Chapter 4 how an axon's output message gets communicated to a downstream neuron's dendrites.

When early anatomists examined slices through the middle of the brain, or when they peeled away the thin layer of the cortex, they discovered a collection of many distinct structures. The tissue immediately beneath the cerebral cortex was fibrous. Because these fibers had the hue and texture of meat fat, they were called *white matter*. Today, we understand that white matter is indeed comprised of fibers, which are the axons of neurons connecting different parts of the brain.

These early anatomists also noted that the cerebral cortex itself, along with various other structures embedded in the white matter, were darker than the white matter, and they called this material *gray matter* (Figure 3.2). Today, we know that this gray matter is comprised of the more or less densely packed cell bodies and

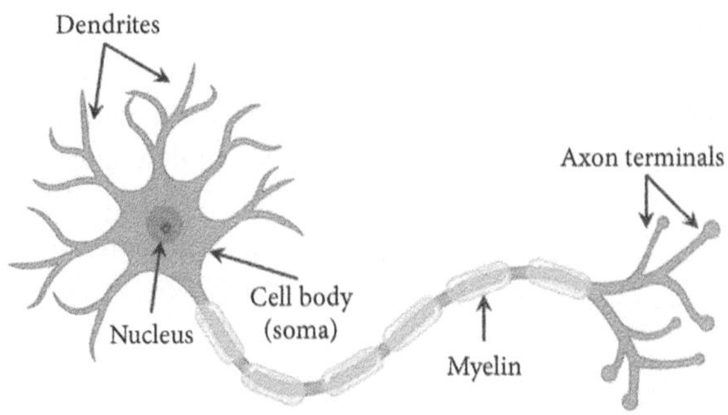

FIGURE 3.1 Neuron structure.

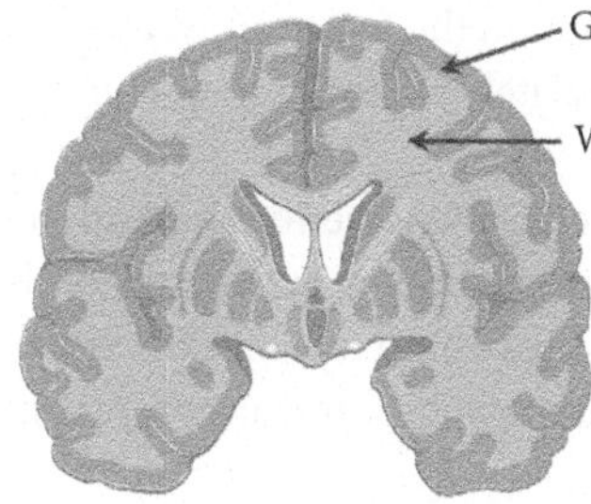

FIGURE 3.2 Cross-section of brain illustrating gray matter and white matter.

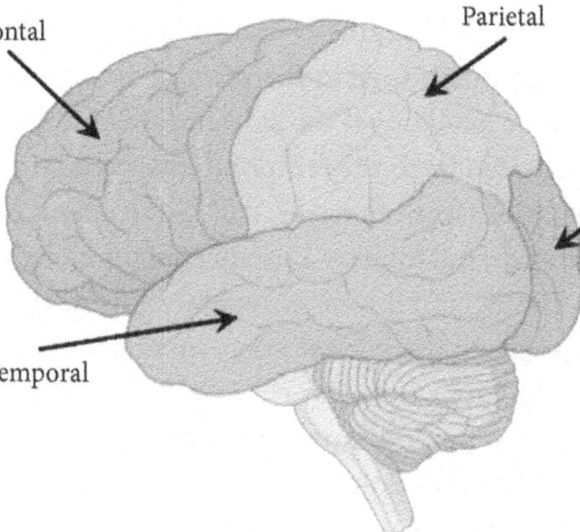

FIGURE 3.3 Lobes of the cerebral cortex.

dendrites of neurons. Collectively, we refer to the gray matter structures beneath the cortex as interior (or *subcortical*) structures, which we will discuss in Chapter 4.

In this chapter, we focus on the gray matter of the cerebral cortex, or "the cortex" for short, which, as we have already seen, is the furrowed outer mantle of the brain. Again, around 90% of that sheet is known as neocortex, or new cortex, referring to its more recent elaboration during the evolution of mammals. The remaining 10% is known as *allocortex* and refers to parts of the cortex that have a less complex structure and are involved in the evolutionary older sense of smell and in memory.

The cortex has two hemispheres, and each is divided by three deep sulci (valleys) into four large parts, or lobes. The lobes appear similar in both hemispheres, though each hemisphere supports somewhat different but often overlapping functions.

The four cortical lobes in each hemisphere are called the *frontal, parietal, occipital,* and *temporal lobes* (Figure 3.3). The brain's lobes are an important part of our locational vocabulary, and references to them appear regularly in litigation over cortical damage and in other health contexts that involve the cortex. Lawyers wanting to represent their clients effectively in cases involving cortical injuries, judges needing to understand those cases, and policymakers trying to understand what the neuroscience of the cortex might imply for policy absolutely must learn to refer to these cortical brain regions confidently. Although the terminology may be new to some readers, these four regions can be readily committed to memory. One easy way to remember them is with the mnemonic device Flower **POT**: FPOT.

- The **frontal lobe** is right behind the forehead, above the eyes.
- The **parietal lobe** is immediately posterior to (behind) the frontal lobe, above the ears.
- The **occipital lobe** is immediately posterior (behind) and ventral to (below) the parietal lobe, sloping down at the back of the brain.
- The **temporal lobe** is roughly behind the cheekbones, ventral to (below) the frontal and parietal lobes, and anterior to (in front of) the occipital lobe.

Although you are unlikely to need a detailed knowledge of all the sulci and gyri, it is important to recognize that the big sulci and gyri, like major rivers geographically dividing states, define the four lobes. The frontal and parietal lobes are separated by the central sulcus, which we mentioned in the prior chapter, a large sulcus running vertically from the top of the head down the side and toward the cheek. The frontal and parietal lobes are separated from the temporal lobe by a large horizontal sulcus that runs anterior to posterior (front to back), called the *lateral sulcus*. The occipital lobe is separated from the parietal lobe by a smaller sulcus called, appropriately, the *parietal-occipital sulcus*. The occipital lobe is separated from the temporal lobe by another prominent sulcus called the *inferior pre-occipital notch*.

Much like geographical regions between rivers or mountains have been divided into politically distinct states, the lobes of the cerebral cortex that are demarcated by major sulci are divided into functionally and structurally distinct areas. Some of the areas are quite well understood, others less so. When we describe the function of the cerebral cortex, we will refer to the functions and relations between these four areas. Particular cortical areas work together to accomplish certain functions, so scientists refer to them collectively as a system or network.

Let's now look in detail at the four cortical lobes, starting at the posterior (back) region of the brain and moving toward the anterior (front).

THE OCCIPITAL LOBE

We begin in the back of the brain because we know most about this lobe, and that knowledge has helped shape our understanding of the other, less understood, lobes. The occipital lobe is the smallest cortical lobe in the human brain. In all mammalian brains it contains the *primary visual cortex*, sometimes also called *V1* or the *striate cortex*, along with other visual areas. The occipital lobe receives information from the eyes, with each visual area generating a map of the visual field in which neighboring points in the image falling on the retina are represented by neighboring locations in the cortex.

Most of the visual cortex represents the central visual field to give you the highest acuity where you are looking. This means that you see less precisely "out of the corner of your eye." Focus your gaze on the "F" at the beginning of this sentence and see how many letters you can read to the right, below, or above. Not very many, right? Yet when you read a sentence naturally, you seem to experience equal visual clarity of all words. This apparent clarity arises through coordination between your visual, eye movement, and memory systems. This clarity is a kind of illusion, though, and can create a sense of confidence in visual perception that is misplaced. Moviemakers have learned to count on this illusory clarity when they design cuts between scenes. The illusory clarity may also have implications for eyewitness testimony.

The fact that the cerebral cortex creates internal maps of the world is a key organizing principle of the brain that we will encounter in many other brain systems. Within these visual maps, visual cortical areas extract the basic features of an image, including location, orientation, depth, color, and shape. This information is conveyed to several other areas in the occipital, parietal, and temporal lobes that extract more refined descriptions of the image, like object form and the direction and speed of a moving object. The process of the brain taking in visual sensory input and making sense of it (visual perception) is referred to by neuroscientists as internally "representing" the external world around you. When witnesses describe what they "saw," they are recalling (or "reconstructing") their internal representation of the external world. (We will turn to the reconstructive nature of memory in Chapter 4.)

Damage to the primary visual cortex results in profound loss of vision. In fact, how the visual world is mapped onto the occipital lobe was worked out by examining where in their visual fields individuals who had suffered localized gunshot wounds to the head could not see. In contrast, damage to other nearby areas causes more subtle problems with visual perception. For example, a particular cortical area contributes to the perception of motion. Lesions to that area don't impair a patient's ability to see an object's shape, color, location, or orientation, but they render the perception of the object's movement through space as a kind of herky-jerky movie. Such patients have difficulty with basic tasks of daily living such as pouring liquids or safely crossing the street. While fortunately rare, this disability illustrates how subtly and powerfully the brain enables, or disables, behavior.

These kinds of conditions seem strange to us precisely because we take for granted the apparently effortless and integrated "view" of the world provided by the visual processing areas in the occipital, parietal, and temporal lobes. This is just one aspect of the general phenomenon that our brains often make more sense of the world than is really there. In addition to being prediction machines, brains are also simplifying machines. They do this both by filling in the gaps of our senses and by filtering out vast amounts of distracting information so that we can attend to the most important signals. When you are reading these words, you are likely unconscious of their font, not to mention oblivious to the sounds of your refrigerator, your dog, or your own blood rushing in your ears.

In addition to our being unconscious of some sensory information, our sensory perception is itself imperfect. Perceptual representations are necessarily distorted in our brains, precisely because they are constructed. Psychologists and neuroscientists delight in discovering new ways in which our brains get things "wrong." Optical illusions are a visual example of this general phenomenon.

Of course, the law is profoundly interested in the limits of our visual perception. In what lighting can a person reliably read a license plate? At what distance can a person reliably distinguish the faces of others? What if the observer and the observed are of different races? What role does experience play in identifying people of other races? What role does stress play in our ability to remember faces?

In short, how good are our visual systems, how do they give rise to biased or distorted perceptions, and what factors impact our ability to accurately remember the images captured by them? The answers to these and many related questions are still being worked out.

THE TEMPORAL LOBE

Although visual information is represented in the occipital lobe, simply decoding the size, shape, and motion of an object is not enough. Human interaction, and thus legal action, requires the brain to *make sense* of those objects. For instance, is the person approaching us a good friend, or just a stranger who looks similar? In its broadest sense, much of the temporal lobe seems to be involved in the recognition and identification of objects, both visual and acoustic, along with the representation of *semantic knowledge*—facts, concepts, and other general knowledge about people, places, and things—that has been gradually acquired across repeated experiences. The temporal lobe's central role in object recognition and *semantic memory* makes it critical for interpreting ongoing experience. In addition, portions of the temporal lobe play a central role in learning and memory for individual experiences, what is termed *episodic memory*. Importantly, depending on the location of injuries to the temporal lobe, one might observe impairments in object recognition, the broad loss of semantic knowledge, or the inability to build and retrieve new episodic memories of life's events.

For example, a part of the temporal lobe called the *fusiform gyrus* is important for a host of visual processing functions, including the ability to sort objects into categories. The fusiform gyrus is important to the legal system because it is also associated with our ability to recognize faces. *Bilateral* (meaning in both hemispheres) injuries to the fusiform gyrus can disrupt our ability to recognize faces (a condition known as prosopagnosia). Disconnection of the fusiform gyrus from other parts of the brain can produce a malady called Capgras syndrome, in which patients do not recognize loved ones, and instead are convinced that their loved ones are being impersonated.

A more general loss of semantic knowledge occurs when the temporal pole—the anterior most portion of the temporal lobe—is injured. The temporal pole serves as a hub or "convergence zone" linking together the various features that constitute a concept or semantic construct. Semantic knowledge supports our understanding of the current state of the world—who we are speaking with, the meanings of the words used in the discussion, and understanding of the various objects and other entities present. Semantic knowledge, like all forms of memory, also provides predictions or expectations that bias our perception and thinking—that is, semantic knowledge helps us interpret the world but also can distort our perceptions of what we think we are seeing or hearing.

Temporal pole damage can be a key issue in brain injury litigation because it is a common consequence of traumatic brain injury (TBI) from car accidents, as this portion of the brain can collide with the inner side of the skull and become injured when the head hits the steering wheel or windshield. Temporal pole impairment also occurs in a progressive form of frontotemporal dementia in which neurodegeneration begins in this region. That form of dementia, termed semantic dementia, is distinct from the more prevalent Alzheimer's disease dementia (which typically first impairs episodic memory, initially leaving semantic memory intact). Be it from TBI, semantic dementia, or another cause, the associated loss of semantic knowledge creates many challenges as individuals are left struggling to interpret the world.

We have considered how the brain processes visual information, but of course we also process auditory information. The temporal lobe is central to our ability to make sense of sound because it contains the *primary auditory cortex*, located on the upper surface of the temporal lobe, tucked into the lateral sulcus. The primary auditory cortex is responsible for extracting characteristics of sound like location, pitch, and frequency modulation. Processing then continues in a sequence of temporal cortical areas located in higher levels of the auditory cortex that resolve the location and identity of sounds. This information is combined with sight and touch to create a coherent multisensory experience used to guide our thoughts and actions.

Whether a witness can accurately pick out the perpetrator's face in a photographic lineup, or really heard the words he thought he heard in the argument between the decedent and his alleged sole heir, are in part questions about the ability of regions in the witness's temporal lobes to recognize and identify objects and sounds and to understand the meanings of experiences. However, even if our perceptions are accurate, our memories about them may be inaccurate. As noted at the outset of this section, other regions in the temporal lobe are central to our ability to build memories for and ultimately remember the individual events we experience in life; we will discuss the role of the hippocampus and other temporal lobe regions in episodic memory in more detail in the next chapter.

THE PARIETAL LOBE

Generally speaking, the parietal lobe's main function is to synthesize the senses of vision, hearing, touch, and balance to guide body movements in space. Circuits in the parietal lobe support your ability to reach for that cup of coffee while holding this book, or to aim that gun accurately before pulling the trigger. Courts have already begun to hear testimony specifically about the parietal lobe on issues of competency, ineffective assistance of counsel, and damages in brain injury litigation.

This synthesizing process begins in a parietal lobe area called the *somatosensory cortex*, which is located at the front (anterior or rostral) edge of the parietal lobe. The somatosensory cortex is responsible for our senses of touch, pain, temperature, and limb position. It contains a map of the body telling us where the touch, pain, or temperature signals are coming from, as well as where our limbs are in space. Like the map in the occipital lobe, the somatosensory map is distorted, with most of the cortical area representing the face, mouth, and fingers. By the way, different sensory nerves convey their messages to different parts of the cortex at different speeds. This explains why, when you hit your thumb with a hammer, your hand recoils before you feel the pain. Sensory messages can travel up to 200 mph; the fastest pain message travels at around 100 mph.

Other areas in the parietal lobe integrate all those sensory inputs into a coherent perception leading to action—"You just stepped on a stone; lift your foot." The integration of these sensory messages is critical to understanding their meaning in the context of our bodies, environment, and goals. Damage to the parietal lobe compromises that perception. For example, stroke patients with damage to certain areas of the parietal lobe in the right hemisphere become cognitively "blind" on the left. They fail to notice objects on the left side of the visual field, even though their eyes and visual pathways are working fine. From a plate full of food they may eat only the portion on the right side, because they only "see" that portion.

In addition to integrating the senses, the parietal lobe integrates more sophisticated aspects of behavior, including action, attention, memory, and language. Stroke patients with damage to areas of the parietal lobe can lose the ability to organize purposeful actions correctly. For example, they might grasp a toothbrush but use it to comb their hair. Their muscles and motor pathways are working fine, but their actions become disorganized. The parietal lobe, along with interconnected regions in the frontal lobe, also supports attention, with one frontoparietal network thought to support the ability to direct attention in a goal-directed manner (e.g., focusing on aspects of an event that are central to achieving a current task or goal) and a second frontoparietal network thought to support the automatic allocation—or capture—of attention by salient stimuli (e.g., the capture of attention by a weapon that may have adverse consequences for encoding the face of the individual wielding it).

Another aspect of organizing actions in sequence and space is the parietal lobe's role in our use of numbers and mathematical reasoning. Neuroimaging studies have found increased activations in the parietal lobe, as well as in some frontal and temporal regions, when people solve math problems. Consider, for example, how natural it feels for the number 7 to be on the "right side" of the number 3, due to our experience with the number line. We represent the ordinal magnitudes of numbers, in part, by drawing on our system that represents spatial positions and spatial relationships.

One especially interesting area of the parietal lobe is the *temporoparietal junction*, or *TPJ*. It is located, eponymously, at the boundary of the temporal and parietal lobes, roughly behind the ear. In addition to having more general attentional functions, the TPJ is a crucial node in a network which scientists call the mentalizing or *Theory of Mind Network*. Other parts of this network include areas in the medial prefrontal cortex. This brain network seems to support our assessment of what other people are thinking, for mentally putting ourselves in their places, a critical ability for a species as intensely social as we.

The law, of course, is very interested not only in how people act but also in the intentions that may lie behind those actions, whether we are talking about a testator's capacity, a witness's competence to testify, or the state of mind of a criminal defendant at the time he committed the offense. Judges and jurors are using their TPJs when making those assessments about the states of mind of others.

We not only use our TPJs to assess a criminal defendant's state of mind at the time of the crime but the TPJ also seems to be involved in integrating that state of mind with the amount of the harm the criminal causes, to produce an assessment of blame. Young children, whose TPJs are not yet fully developed, adults with lesions in the TPJ, and volunteer subjects who have their TPJs experimentally disrupted by brain stimulation, all assess accidental harms as being more blameworthy than attempted harms. To them, no harm means no foul. Because they lack fully functioning TPJs, they are either missing the signals of intentionality, or perhaps are simply unable to integrate those signals into an assessment of blame. As a result, they cannot appreciate that someone who shoots purposefully but misses is morally (and legally) more culpable than someone who shoots accidentally and kills.

Other areas of the parietal lobe are involved with oral and written language comprehension, including the well-known *Wernicke's area*, a cortical region located at the posterior end of the superior temporal gyrus, a large roughly diagonal gyrus straddling the temporal and parietal lobes. Wernicke's area is usually differentially active in the language dominant hemisphere (left side for right-handed people). Damage to Wernicke's area can cause a particular kind of language impairment. In the simplest terms, patients can hear spoken words and sentences but are unable to understand them even though they can produce speech. Such patients will also produce sequences of words to make sentences that don't make sense or make up words that have no meaning but be unaware of these mistakes.

THE FRONTAL LOBE

In humans, the frontal lobe is the largest, supporting our unique ability to behave flexibly, navigate complex social relationships, communicate using symbols through speech, art, and music, contemplate mindboggling options, and plan further into the future and organize more complex activities than any other species on the planet.

Anatomically, the frontal lobe has a top and a bottom plus the medial surface. The top is organized in four strips—a posterior one running mediolaterally (side to side) and three running rostrocaudally (front to back)—corresponding to the four gyri (hills) from which the four parts take their name: precentral; superior frontal; middle frontal; and inferior frontal. Functionally, the frontal lobe is commonly divided into three broad areas: the primary motor cortex (in the posterior part of the precentral gyrus); the secondary motor cortex (in the anterior part of the precentral gyrus); and the prefrontal cortex (everything else) (Figure 3.4).

Our tour begins on top. The *primary motor cortex*, also called the motor strip, is located in the central sulcus at the posterior (back) end of the frontal lobe, immediately rostral to (in front of) the somatosensory cortex. It is involved in producing articulated, skilled, voluntary movements of the body, such as speaking, writing, or typing. Certain neurons in the primary motor cortex pass through the brainstem and spinal cord and ultimately communicate with the neurons in the spinal cord that activate the body's muscles. These connections form a rough map of the body

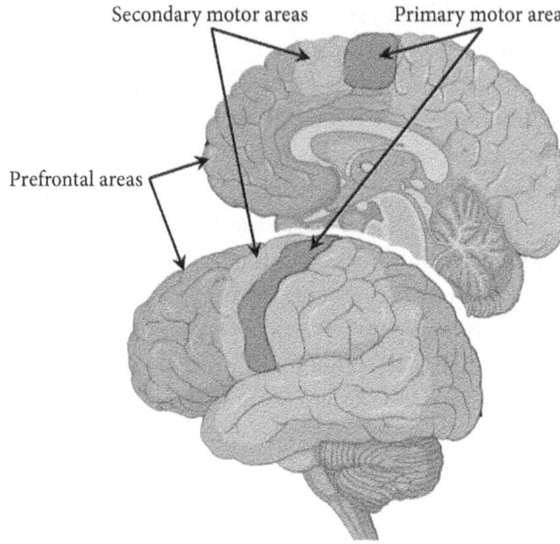

FIGURE 3.4 Regions of the frontal lobe.

in the primary motor cortex, complementing and corresponding to the sensory body map found in the somatosensory cortex.

When a signal is received by the primary motor cortex to, for example, "grasp this page between your left thumb and index finger, then turn the page," the neurons in the hand region of primary motor cortex organize the pattern of muscles to be activated with proper sequence and strength to accomplish that movement. The nerve impulses flow from the cerebral cortex into the spinal cord, causing the muscles to contract. It is worth pausing to appreciate the amazing amplification that happens in this (seemingly) simple process of turning the page. The volition to turn the page was converted through nerves and muscles into a force acting on an object in the world. The amplification can be as delicate as a caress or as powerful as a punch.

The *secondary motor cortex,* which is divided into a lateral *premotor area* and medial *supplementary motor area,* is located immediately anterior or rostral to (in front of) the primary motor cortex and is responsible for organizing, planning, and coordinating sequences of movements guided by the environment and volition. In the "turn the page" example, the secondary motor cortex would be involved in planning and coordinating the sequence of the movements needed to accomplish the grasping and the turning of the page, while also reaching for the drink placed beside you and glancing out the window.

Researchers have discovered neurons in the motor areas (as well as other areas in the parietal lobe) that signal not only the production of an action but also the mere observation of that action. For example, a portion of the neurons that are active before we grasp an object will also be active when we view another person grasping that object. Called *mirror neurons,* these have been theorized to be fundamental to the brain circuits enabling theory of mind, which in turn allows us to understand the actions of others and to empathize.

Neuroscientists and physicians have learned how to implant arrays of sensors (part of a *brain-machine interface* or *BMI,* sometimes *BCI* for brain-computer interface) that detect the nerve impulses in the primary and secondary motor cortices of individuals who suffer paralysis, so that these people can move robotic arms. With practice, the patients can learn to move the robotic arms sometimes as effortlessly as you move yours. Brain-machine interfaces like this are used to treat some movement disorders, and they may become more common. Many ethical and legal issues are raised by these devices, including who "owns" the BMI device and who is responsible for its upkeep.

The *prefrontal cortex*, or *PFC*, refers to the expanse of the frontal lobe lying immediately anterior or rostral (in front of) the secondary motor cortex. It is the frontmost part of the frontal cortex and forms much of the crowning forehead in the human brain. Neuroscientists recognize this part of the brain is essential for the most complex of cognitive functions. Not surprisingly, scientists understand this large region least of all. You can think of the PFC as the "CEO" of the brain, being richly connected ultimately with many other parts of the cerebral cortex and interacting with the structures beneath the cerebral cortex discussed in Chapter 4. In the PFC, representations from all of the senses plus memories are combined with emotions and motivations to form goals that lead to the production of extended sequences of movements, such as typing this sentence. The PFC supports the most complex kinds of behavior, including abstraction, foresight, planning, risk-assessment, inhibition, and decision-making. Extensive research has confirmed that the PFC is crucial for the ability to do many of the higher order things we do that make us human, including being able to pay or shift attention, delay gratification, stay motivated, assess risks and benefits, foresee multiple possible futures, and choose between several courses of action, rather than simply responding in a habitual manner.

Because of its role in deliberation, decision-making, and volition, the PFC is central to the brain networks most relevant to law, and therefore the cortical region on which we will spend most of our time. The PFC is typically divided into five parts: (1) dorsolateral PFC (or DLPFC, located on the upper side of the PFC); (2) ventrolateral PFC (or VLPFC, located on the lower side of PFC); (3) frontopolar cortex (or FPC, located at the anterior pole of the frontal lobe); (4) medial PFC (or MPFC, or just MFC, located in the middle of the brain, above the nose); and (5) orbital PFC (or OFPFC, or just OFC, located on the bottom of the frontal lobe, above the eyes) (Figure 3.5). While progress is being made in understanding the functions of frontopolar cortex, including its role in representing higher-order goals, planning, problem-solving, and episodic memory, here we will focus on the other four areas.

Dorsolateral Prefrontal Cortex (DLPFC)

The overall function of the DLPFC can be understood as *executive control*—the capacity to act according to consequences and goals—and *fluid intelligence*—the capacity to reason, solve unique problems, and guide actions. These entail more basic capacities such as goal-directed guiding of attention (focusing on this book and not that cell phone), *working memory* (remembering an address or phone number or keeping in mind the elements of a problem to solve), identifying categories, representing cues, rules, and task sets (governing actions by representing relevant

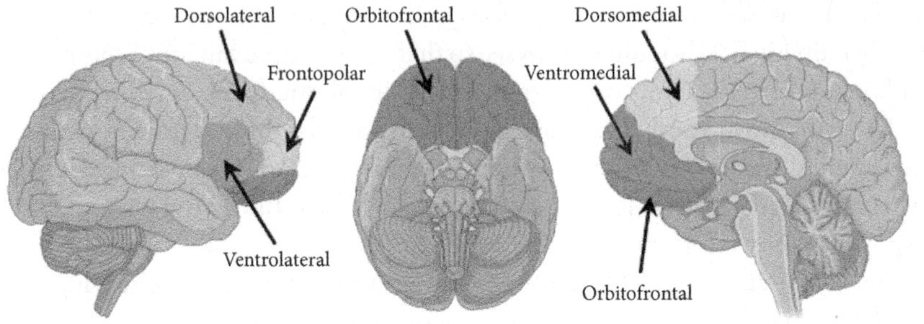

FIGURE 3.5 Areas of the prefrontal cortex.

stimulus dimensions and their mappings to the appropriate actions given the task), and making decisions (resolving among alternatives based on goals and values). The DLPFC is crucial to our ability to think abstractly and hypothetically, to plan, and to entertain counterfactuals. This enables us to anticipate and simulate events that might or might not happen in the future. These DLPFC functions support our ability to engage in the conscious prediction that is so critical to our species. Should I breach that contract, contest that will, file a lawsuit for personal injuries, or stab that aggressor? Will that load of fruit rot if I wait one more day to ship it, will that person die if I shoot him in the leg? Legislators, regulators, judges, lawyers, parties, parole boards—all decision makers in the legal system—use their DLPFC to make predictions. For example, recent experiments have shown that the DLPFC is crucial to the judgments that subjects make when they impose punishments on hypothetical criminals. These functions of the DLPFC improve through adolescence and mature in the middle of the third decade of life, and indeed this developmental trajectory has been the basis for many arguments about juvenile criminal responsibility.

Ventrolateral Prefrontal Cortex (VLPFC)

The VLPFC contributes to multiple functions, including working memory, using goals to accomplish tasks, and handling aspects of language. The posterior part of the VLPFC is associated with language, including production and syntax. *Broca's area*—named after Pierre Paul Broca, who discovered its role in language in the nineteenth century—is necessary for the production of language, as distinguished from the already mentioned Wernicke's area, which is necessary for the comprehension of language. Like many functions of the human cerebral cortex, the language functions supported by the left and right hemispheres are different. As with Wernicke's area, Broca's area is typically located in the dominant hemisphere (left side for right-handed people); however, the corresponding region in the other hemisphere contributes the rhythms of prosody to speech. Beyond contributions to language, other research indicates that the middle and anterior parts of the VLPFC, together with other structures in dorsal parietal cortex and elsewhere, support the representation of task goals and the selection of inputs or memories that are relevant to achieving those goals. Research also indicates that, together with the TPJ in the parietal lobe, the VLPFC signals the occurrence of important (salient) stimuli that demand attention and interruption of ongoing action.

Medial Prefrontal Cortex (MPFC)

The MPFC consists of dorsal (toward the crown) regions and ventral (toward the chin) regions. The dorsal region (DMPFC), which neighbors and is associated with the anterior cingulate cortex (discussed later), has been associated with several complex functions. One function is self-monitoring by recognizing the consequences of one's own actions, which is central to the feeling that one is responsible for one's own actions. Relatedly, the DMPFC is also associated with self-control of actions and emotions. Other research shows that the DMPFC is involved with social cognition, theory of mind (with the parietal lobe), and moral decision-making based on empathy or altruism.

The ventral region (VMPFC), which neighbors and is associated with the orbital frontal cortex (discussed later), has been associated with cost–benefit analysis and risk assessment to evaluate alternative actions, and with the regulation of emotion. Its role in emotion regulation is believed to be enabled through connections with an interior structure called the amygdala (discussed in the next chapter). These functions are manifest particularly in situations that involve the assessment of moral and legal blame. These judgments are in turn informed by assessments of the amount of harm caused and the intention of the wrongdoer. The VMPFC, along with the TPJ, seems to play a key role in integrating harm and intention into blame, which, as we saw previously, is then used by the DLPFC to make a punishment decision. Patients with bilateral lesions of the VMPFC have normal intellectual ability but commonly exhibit impaired personal and social decision-making. Such individuals tend to prefer most immediately rewarding options and are insensitive to consequences.

Orbital Frontal Cortex (OFC)

The OFC includes areas that mediate our sense of smell. It potently guides behavior toward preferable items and away from disgusting or undesirable ones. Working with the VMPFC and interior structures known as the *limbic system* (described in Chapter 4), the OFC contributes to valuing basic rewards like food and drink, reflecting individual preferences, and also with the act of punishing. It also contributes to our ability to appreciate predictive cues that motivate actions leading to basic rewards, like whether there's food hiding in that moving bush. Because such actions predicted by the OFC might include withholding a movement (be still until that rabbit exits the bush), the OFC contributes to self-control. OFC function also applies to more abstract rewards like money or social status.

CORTICAL REGIONS THAT SPAN LOBES

In addition to the brain's four lobes, there are two important cortical areas that lie across or sit between the lobes—the insula and the cingulate cortex (Figure 3.6).

Insula

Buried in the lateral sulcus of the brain is a cortical region known as the insula, which runs in an anterior-posterior direction and sits between the temporal, parietal, and frontal lobes. Being less accessible than other cortical regions, less is known about the insula, which includes anterior and posterior segments and, as noted previously, up to thirteen distinct areas. In recent decades, functional neuroimaging studies have found increased activation of the insula during a diverse variety of conditions and tasks. The insula is highly relevant to many legal issues, because when you "follow your gut" in deciding an uncertain course of action, or ruminate with stomach-churning, heart-racing, dry-throat anxiety, or agonize about how much the visit to the dentist will hurt, or feel someone else's pain, or contemplate moral dilemmas, you can thank your insula for linking internal body states to difficult or uncertain external situations and resulting actions.

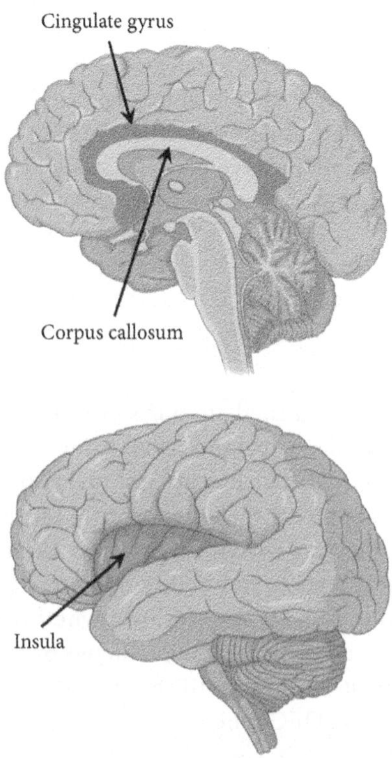

FIGURE 3.6 Cingulate cortex and insula (also showing corpus callosum).

We will describe three broad functions supported by the insula. These diverse functions are enabled through connections with cortical areas in the medial frontal (in particular the anterior cingulate cortex, described later), orbital frontal (in particular, olfactory), parietal (in particular, somatosensory areas), and temporal lobes.

First, the insula contributes to the perception of internal body states and *autonomic* responses to those states. Neuroimaging indicates that insula activity increases when participants become aware of thirst, heartbeat, or distention of the esophagus, stomach, bladder, or rectum. The insula is also essential for pain perception. Neuroimaging studies associate increased activation of the insula with perception of heat/cold and the severity of painful stimulation. Damage to or removal of the insula can result in reduced or altered pain perception. The insula is directly involved in processing the intensity, quality, and affective value of taste stimuli, as well as anticipating and attending to tastes and smells.

Second, being a central node in responding to visceral signals about the body, the insula is thought to play a crucial role in arousal and subjective feelings associated with emotions. Neuroimaging studies have found increased activations of the insula upon viewing disgusting, frightening, happy, sad, or sexual images. Damage to the insula can result in abnormal experience of emotion, apathy, or anxiety. Through its role in self-awareness of internal body states, the insula is also critical for recognition of emotion in others and empathy supporting social interaction. It is thus an important part of the Theory of Mind Network. Neuroimaging studies describe increased activation of the insula upon viewing expressions of pain, disgust, fear, anxiety, or happiness in others. Indeed, the insula supports feelings of disgust at unfairness in economic or similar exchanges, including norm violations. This capacity is altered or eliminated following damage to the insula.

Third, the insula contributes to responding appropriately to multiple, conflicting internal and external stimuli. In neuroimaging studies with tasks that require careful consideration and self-control, the insula is one of the most commonly observed increased activations, usually in association with the DLPFC, the VLPFC, and the anterior cingulate cortex, a region we discuss next. With its representations of internal body states and connections with the OFC, the insula is thought to contribute to decision-making under risk and uncertainty. When reason cannot resolve alternatives, then emotions, hunches, and the gut lead the way. Indeed, neuroimaging studies report increased activation of the insula during experimental tasks requiring responses under risk, uncertainty, and conflicting impulses, often in parallel with anterior cingulate cortex. Damage to the insula can impair decision-making in these conditions.

Cingulate Cortex

On the medial surface of the brain, adjacent and ventral to (under) the frontal and parietal lobes, is a gyrus (hill) that loops like a belt on top of the corpus callosum, the large crescent-shaped bundle of nerves that connects the two hemispheres around the base of the brain (Figure 3.6). From the Latin term for belt, "cingulum," it is called the *cingulate cortex*. Based on its connections, neuroscientists initially emphasized the relationship of the cingulate cortex with the limbic system of the brain (a collection of structures mediating emotion and memory, covered in Chapter 4). However, we now recognize that different parts of cingulate cortex contribute to distinct functions. The cingulate cortex is another region—or, more precisely, set of regions—implicated in various legally relevant issues like assessing harm, evaluating risk, assigning guilt, and formulating lies.

The cingulate cortex is traditionally divided into front and back parts, the *anterior cingulate cortex* (ACC) and the *posterior cingulate cortex* (PCC). Both parts of the cingulate cortex are connected to the cortex above and to structures below that enable the expression and regulation of emotions. The density of these connections is one important piece of evidence suggesting that the traditional dichotomy between emotion and cognition may be oversimplified.

The ACC in particular has been shown to be involved not only in the regulation of emotion but also in the ever important and seemingly "cognitive" role of assessing risks and benefits between prospective actions. In experiments involving one kind of decision-making—how much to punish hypothetical criminals—the cingulate cortex, along with the other cortical regions described previously—was increasingly engaged during the assessment of harm and of intention. The ACC was more involved in the assessment of harm, and the PCC, being part of the Theory of Mind Network, was more involved in the assessment of the wrongdoer's intention.

The cingulate cortex's rich connections with other areas associated with memory (principally the hippocampus, Chapter 4) likewise suggest that memory may be something much richer than a mere recording of past events. Memory has a significant reconstructive, or narrative, aspect. It is less like a video recorder and more like a storyteller, who keeps telling, retelling, and often changing the stories.

The cingulate cortex (with the insula) is also involved in sensing and reacting to pain. As we will see in Chapter 9, the brain senses pain through pathways that are distinct from the standard somatosensory system responsible for our sense of touch and limb positions. In humans, pain signals reach the cerebral cortex in the insula and the ACC. The insula's role in mentally representing the state of the body is believed to give it the capacity for conscious awareness of painful or uncomfortable states of the body. The anterior cingulate cortex is believed to regulate the response to a painful stimulus. For example, you are less likely to drop an expensive china cup than an inexpensive one when boiling hot tea spills on your hand.

Finally, and relatedly, the ACC also contributes to signaling when decisions are difficult ("painful decision"), when one makes an error, or when the consequences of one's actions are unexpected. Of legal relevance, when experimental participants are instructed to fabricate a lie, the ACC and the insula become very active, though it is far too simplistic to say that lies can be reliably detected just by measuring the activities in these two regions. This is, in part, because the function of any given brain region at any specific moment in time depends heavily on the set of other regions with which it is currently interacting. We will discuss in Chapter 10 the likelihood that improved neuroimaging techniques might someday be able to detect lies reliably.

CONNECTING THE LOBES

Each of the four lobes of the cortex—frontal, parietal, occipital, and temporal—are sophisticated areas of brain processing, with each consisting of many functionally distinct regions that are part of multiple, distinct brain networks. Indeed, it would be a mistake to think of each lobe (or region) as operating independently of the rest of the brain. In the brain, no area is an island. Although there is some localization of function, no area in the cerebral cortex has just one function. Each area is interconnected to other cortical areas as well as with numerous interior structures (see Chapter 4). Hence, as noted before, modern neuroscience speaks of "networks" not centers, and this is meant to capture the reality that function emerges from brain networks that involve populations of neurons in multiple lobes plus interior structures influencing each other simultaneously.

We close this chapter with two illustrations of how brain areas can work together to enable functions. There are other legally relevant networks, but we hope this introduction to these two—the language network and the risk-reward network—will help give you a flavor of the complexities of these interactions.

The Language Network

Language depends on multiple types of representations and processes, along with dynamic interactions between them. The dominant classical view of how the brain enables language focused on three structures as particularly essential: Wernicke's area in the posterior temporal and ventral parietal lobes (for language comprehension); Broca's area in the frontal lobe (for language production); and a large bundle of nerve cell axons, called the *arcuate fasciculus* or, more colloquially, "the language loop," that connects Wernicke's area with Broca's area. But discoveries over the past thirty years indicate that this model is far too simplistic.

First, it is now known that there are at least two distinct pathways in these connections—a deeper one that appears to connect Wernicke's and Broca's directly (a kind of express bus) and a shallower one that has two segments (a kind of local bus). Damage to these different pathways can cause different kinds of language dysfunction, from an inability to speak at all (aphasia) to stuttering.

Second, a well of evidence now indicates that other structures also contribute to key aspects of language. For example, the act of reading text aloud requires, among other things, the perception of visual word forms in the ventral occipital-temporal cortex, the activation of different components of speech-based processes in ventrolateral prefrontal, premotor and motor cortex, and in the cerebellum, all of which interact to ultimately support saying the words, along with activation of the words' associated semantics via interactions with the temporal pole and inferior parietal lobule. Perhaps for this reason, it's now understood that patients can demonstrate deficits consistent with Broca's aphasia even without damage to Broca's area, reflecting the consequences of disrupting other structures that, together with Broca's areas, support language production.

Third, there is increasing evidence that there are even more finely specified cognitive and linguistic parts of the language network, which, for example, can distinguish between phonological (sounds) and syntactic (grammar) components of language. The field is actively working to build more comprehensive models of the brain regions, networks, and their interactions that support language.

The Risk-Reward Network

The basic decision to approach or avoid based on risks and rewards is fundamental to life. A network formed by parts of the cerebral cortex together with the collection of structures known as the *basal ganglia* (see Chapter 4) is crucial to the ability to learn from consequences and select effective actions. This network begins with *corticostriatal pathways,* named after their origin in the cortex and terminus in the *striatum,* an interior structure that functions as the input region of the basal ganglia. Known colloquially as the *risk-reward network,* this network is critical to the brain's primary evolutionary task of assessing the environment and then making decisions based on a prediction of risks and rewards.

This network cannot function accurately without a *neurotransmitter* called *dopamine* (explained in Chapter 4). The release of dopamine in this network, from neurons originating in the midbrain, is associated with the feeling of pleasure. Roughly, the dopamine network seems to measure expected gains (How good will it feel to take and keep all the money in this bank's safe?) against expected costs (Will I get caught, and, if so, how will I be punished?) in order to guide behavior. Significantly, the risk-reward network recalibrates expected gains in a way that prevents most of us from sitting around all day eating potato chips or having sex. Defects in this "been there done that" feature may be central to understanding the mystery of addiction and both of its central aspects—difficulty abstaining and the need for increased doses.

***

Many legally relevant brain structures sit beneath the cortex, several of which are not only part of the brain's conscious decision-making but also provide important emotional shortcuts to that decision-making. We turn in the next chapter to an exploration of these interior structures.

4

THE INTERIOR OF THE BRAIN

Ben and Kristi Reavis were driving their Lexus sedan in downtown Dallas, their two children, aged three and five, buckled in car seats in the back. They were stopped in traffic when they were rear-ended by a man driving an SUV at an impact speed of almost 50 mph. Ben and Kristi suffered only minor injuries, but the impact drove their front seats back into the children. Both children lost consciousness, sustained skull fractures, underwent neurosurgeries, and suffered permanent brain damage. They eventually recovered most of their physical functioning, but their neurosurgeon testified that both suffered diffuse axonal shearing, a tearing of axons across the brain. Each child lost all memories of their prior lives. They did not know who their parents were, or any of their friends or other relatives, and had no memories of the home they lived in for their short lives. They had to begin making new memories once they regained consciousness. They began having significant never-before-seen behavioral issues at home and at school. The Reavises sued the car manufacturer as well as its related sales and distribution company, and a jury awarded them $98 million in compensatory damages and $92 million in punitive damages, against both defendants jointly and severally. The judgment was affirmed as against the manufacturer but reversed as against the sales and distribution company.

Toyota Motors Sales, Inc. v. Reavis,
627 S.W.3d 713 (Tex. App. 2021).

INTRODUCTION

Immediately beneath the cerebral cortex is a white, fatty, fibrous tissue that is comprised of the axons to and from the neurons in the cerebral cortex connecting them with each other and with the interior regions we will now discuss. These interior regions are dense collections of neuron cell bodies and associated dendrites.

Brain Science for Lawyers, Judges, and Policymakers. Owen D. Jones, Jeffrey D. Schall, Francis X. Shen, Morris B. Hoffman and Anthony D. Wagner, Oxford University Press. © Oxford University Press 2024.
DOI: 10.1093/oso/9780197748855.003.0004

They have a variety of shapes and appearances, driven by differences in their connections and functions.

These structures are central to both legal practice and doctrine. Your ability as a lawyer to remember the facts of your case requires the hippocampus, which is part of the allocortex, the evolutionarily older layer of the cortex immediately below the neocortex. A judge's emotions when rendering a sentence are mediated, in part, by the amygdala, another interior structure. The interplay between the hippocampus, amygdala, and additional structures produce signals that guide many forms of decision-making.

As with the cerebral cortex, neuroscientists divide the brain's interior structures on the basis of both their structure and function, and we will do the same. After briefly describing the thalamus, we will restrict ourselves to considering two functional systems in these deep structures—the limbic system and the basal ganglia—and we will sample six of the many anatomically distinct structures that lie in one or the other of these two systems. In the limbic system, we will look at the hippocampus, amygdala, hypothalamus, and pituitary gland; and in the basal ganglia, we will look at the striatum and substantia nigra. But first, we pause to consider an important interior structure that straddles the limbic and basal ganglia groupings: the thalamus.

THALAMUS

The *thalamus* is an egg-shaped collection of neurons at the bottom center of the brain, near the brainstem. "Thalamus" is Latin for "egg." It is so richly connected to the brainstem that some anatomists consider the thalamus to be a continuation of the brainstem. The thalamus is composed of multiple parts, referred to as nuclei (not to be confused with cell nuclei). As with the cortical lobes discussed in the prior chapter, and the other interior structures we discuss in the rest of this chapter, the thalamus appears in each hemisphere, though its location smack in the middle of the brain means that its two sides are next to one another.

The first thing to understand about the thalamus is that its neurons relay their inputs to the cerebral cortex. The second thing to understand is that each part of the thalamus receives unique inputs; some of those inputs are derived from the sense organs, and others are derived from other parts of the brain. The third thing to understand is that different parts of the thalamus are connected to different parts of the cerebral cortex. Thus, for example, cortical areas that perform visual processing receive inputs from parts of the thalamus that receive inputs from neurons in the retina of the eye. Cortical areas that contribute to body movements receive inputs from parts of the thalamus that receive inputs from the cerebellum and basal ganglia, which are responsible for coordinating movements.

The thalamus is thus a kind of routing station responsible for directing a specific type of sensory and other input to appropriate areas of the cortex. A loss of oxygen supply to different parts of the thalamus will therefore result in an impairment or complete loss of different functions.

LIMBIC SYSTEM

"Limbic" is Latin for "border." The term was used by early anatomists to describe a collection of structures encircling the thalamus and brainstem. As more structures were discovered and functions parsed, the term "limbic" has lost much of its descriptive appeal, and some neuroscientists don't use the term at all. But old habits are hard to break, and because many neuroscientists continue to describe this system as the *limbic* system, you should be familiar with the term.

Of its many functions, it is most important to note for legal purposes that the limbic system is associated with memory and emotion. We will cover four important structures in the limbic system: the hippocampus, which is associated with certain kinds of memory; the amygdala, which is associated with certain kinds of emotion; and the hypothalamus and the pituitary gland, which regulate the internal state of the body and brain (Figure 4.1).

Although these structures are in the limbic system and are distinct anatomically from the cortical structures described in Chapter 3, we remind readers that the brain is highly interconnected. It would be grossly oversimplified to say that "memories are stored in the hippocampus" or that the amygdala is the brain's "emotion center"—claims we have seen occasionally in the popular press and in legal contexts.

Hippocampus

The limbic structure thought to be primarily associated with memory for events and facts is the *hippocampus*. The word is Greek for "sea horse," to which it shares a stunning resemblance. The hippocampus is located in the medial portion of the temporal lobe. Through interactions with medial temporal and prefrontal cortex, it contributes mainly to a particular kind of memory called *episodic memory*. This type

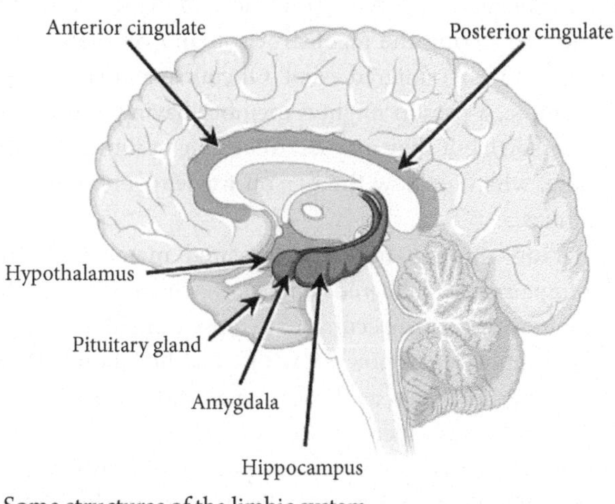

FIGURE 4.1 Some structures of the limbic system.

of memory supports conscious remembering of experienced personal episodes and other events, as well as the ability to recognize a stimulus (such as a face) as having been previously encountered. Episodic memory is distinct from *semantic memory*, which is the memory for facts and concepts—about the world, about others, and even about the self—which is acquired through multiple learning experiences and stored across multiple cortical regions. Episodic memory is also distinct from a third, nonconscious, form of memory called *procedural memory*, which encodes, stores, and retrieves the procedures (rather than episodes) that underlie motor, visuospatial, or cognitive skills, such as how to ride a bike. Procedural memory is supported by the second subcortical network we will describe later, the basal ganglia.

The association of the hippocampus with episodic memory became evident when scientists discovered that a patient treated for epilepsy—through removing the hippocampus (and surrounding structures) from both hemispheres of his brain—suffered a profound inability to form new memories of events. Such a disorder is known as *anterograde amnesia*. Many readers will be familiar with anterograde amnesia, as it is the central early symptom in Alzheimer's disease. In fact, Alzheimer's is associated with the accumulation of tau protein "tangles" in a part of the cortex that provides the majority of inputs to the hippocampus. The spread of these tangles into the hippocampus begins to impair function, leading to difficulties in building and retrieving new episodic memories. Damage to the medial temporal lobe, including the hippocampus, also can be the result of other causes, including traumatic brain injury following forces to the skull (such as due to explosions or head injuries in a car accident) or hypoxia (a sustained period of inadequate oxygenation).

The hippocampus is thought to play such a central role in the building of new episodic memories because it is the only brain structure that receives inputs from the many other brain regions that represent the various elements of an event (e.g., the who, what, where, and when). In essence, the hippocampus is the brain region that can hear all of the different pieces of an orchestra, and its role during an event is to bind together which pieces are playing and where they are positioned at that moment. By storing a neural trace of the who, what, where, and when of an event, the hippocampus enables recalling of the event at some point in the future. Remembering occurs when a cue (one piece of the orchestra) reactivates the hippocampal trace, triggering the reconstruction and reinstatement of the other pieces of the previously encountered event. Of course, remembering is not always complete; for example, a person might remember having encountered a piece of an event (e.g., a person), but they may fail to be able to remember the other event details (e.g., where, when, or how the person was encountered), a phenomenon termed source amnesia.

While anterograde amnesia refers to impaired memory for new events, a second striking impairment, *retrograde amnesia*—which refers to the loss of previously made memories—also occurs with hippocampal damage. Importantly, previously stored memories are not lost with equal likelihood; instead, the most recently formed memories (such as those learned just prior to the neural injury) are more often lost, whereas older memories (such as those from childhood) are less likely to be lost. Scientists interpret this pattern of retrograde amnesia as evidence that while episodic memories initially depend on the hippocampus, over time they are "consolidated" outside of the hippocampus and thus eventually become hippocampal independent. Scientists call this form of memory consolidation *systems consolidation*, as the suggestion is that a memory's dependence shifts from one brain system based primarily in the hippocampus to another system distributed across cortical structures.

While this all might sound complex, there is considerable relevance for the law. For example, families and the courts are frequently asked to wrestle with the fact that an individual in early stages of Alzheimer's disease might fail to remember a conversation that occurred just moments ago, while being able to remember events from years prior in rich details. What are the implications for judgments of competency or duress? And what do we know about what's likely in store for the individual going forward? Unfortunately, as Alzheimer's disease advances, it impacts cortical structures beyond the hippocampus, which leads to the progressive loss of older memories along with a loss of semantic memory; the latter often results in the inability to recognize well-known family members, common objects, and the meaning of words.

At the other end of life, infantile amnesia refers to the inability to remember events that occurred during the first three years of age. In contrast to anterograde and retrograde amnesia, which are the consequences of brain injury or neurodegenerative disease, we all experience infantile amnesia as a consequence of functional changes in our brains that occur over the early years of life. This has obvious implications whenever the law is asked to reach back to a party or victim's first three years or so of childhood, such as in cases alleging abuse or sex assault against a young child who is now an adult.

As we've already mentioned, our memories are not replicas like a video recording. The processes of consolidating and retrieving long-term memories are affected by the context in which they occur. How we represent an event, and thus what we store in memory, is influenced by our interpretations of the event as it unfolds, what our goals are at the time, which aspects of the event we attend to, among other factors. In addition, each act of remembering leads to learning of what we recalled, which itself can alter future remembering. Thus, the second retrieval of a memory will be different from the first, just because it occurs during a different kind of intra-brain conversation and because the first recall altered memory. In other words, episodic remembering—including about our own autobiography or about things like how vivid our memory was when initially picking someone out of a lineup—often entails a kind of storytelling or confabulation. This reconstruction of memories, shaped by both what actually happened along with our beliefs about what happened and our goals at the time of remembering, can lead to false or distorted memories, including confident recollections of events that didn't happen as recalled or at all.

But we do not wish to overstate the fragility of memory. Overall, the brain is a remarkable retrieval machine, and for good evolutionary reasons. Our early ancestors would not have survived if they couldn't remember to avoid poisonous plants or dangerous animals. The important point is that memories are not perfect because they are not recordings. The extent to which they are not accurate reflections of events seems to depend on many factors, including the individual experiencing the event, the content and context of the event or fact being learned, and all the circumstances of the remembering.

Of course, being able to distinguish between experiences to remember and experiences to forget is an essential function of memory. Brains that remembered everything—including those refrigerator noises and barking dogs—would create real challenges, as memory for the irrelevant or trivial would interfere with and overwhelm our ability to remember the more important aspects of life. There are three kinds of experiences we really need to remember.

The first are those that are motivationally significant or meaningful to us, which can lead us to reason our way into deciding we should try to remember them, such as the date of your wedding anniversary or the name of someone you just met at a party whom you find interesting.

The second type of experiences we really need to remember are those that are surprising or unexpected; as we've noted, our memory systems confer value because they provide predictive models of the world that are built on past experience. As a consequence, experiences that are unexpected—that is, the event is novel in some way, violating our current world model—are more informative and thus they should be better remembered. Our brains have built-in mechanisms that increase the likelihood that we will build and stabilize memories of the novel or unexpected.

The third type of need-to-remember memories are those that may have been so important for our survival that they are emotionally tagged with a kind of "remember this for future reference" label, such as when we pull the sheets back and find a snake in our bed, or walk around the corner and see a gun pointed in our face. Cognition and emotion both contribute to the nature and depth of our consolidated memories, mediated by the rich connections of the hippocampus to the cortex above and to emotional regions below.

Motivation, novelty, and arousal processes not only impact systems consolidation but also affect a second, more rapid form of consolidation—termed *cellular consolidation*—which results in the strengthening of the synapses between the neurons that constitute a hippocampal trace for an experience. This form of consolidation is time-dependent, playing out during the hours after an experience, and can be disrupted by certain pharmacological compounds. Within legal settings, amnesia due to disrupted cellular consolidation may be encountered in cases related to "date rape drugs" or other drugs, and the excessive consumption of alcohol.

The hippocampus is particularly sensitive to stress, though the relationship between the two is still not entirely understood. Acute stress can impact the hippocampus along with prefrontal cortical function, which affects how episodic memories are laid down. Such stress during an event can increase the likelihood that the stress-inducing features of the event (such as a gun) are encoded and consolidated in memory, but decrease the likelihood that other event features (such as the perpetrator's face) are stored.

Acute stress at the time of retrieval, on the other hand, appears to be generally disruptive, decreasing the probability of being able to remember past events. It is therefore not at all uncommon for some (but not all) victims of trauma to suffer gaps in their memory of the traumatic event; such gaps could be due to stress-induced disruptions of what is encoded or disruptions of retrieval processes, or both. Importantly, the disruptive effects of stress on memory retrieval can provide a biological account for why a victim may fail to remember some aspects of a traumatic experience when memory is probed right after—and stress levels remain high—but then can remember those additional details later—when stress levels have dampened. Deviations in a victim's statements across two instances of remembering aren't necessarily a sign of unreliability or memory errors—the challenge for the law is knowing which deviations result in a more complete and accurate memory for what transpired and which reflect memory distortions or motivated acts by the rememberer.

Chronic stress, including that experienced in conditions like post-traumatic stress disorder (PTSD), can also degrade the hippocampus's ability to build, consolidate, and retrieve memories. Animal studies have shown that chronic stress can actually degrade the neural connections in the hippocampus, and human and animal work also reveals reductions in hippocampal volume; these and other stress effects may result in more global impairments in an individual's memory function.

While we have focused on the role of the hippocampus in episodic memory, we also know that the hippocampus plays an important role in representing space and guiding navigation, building "cognitive maps" that integrate across experience to represent the world. Animal studies have demonstrated that neurons in the hippocampus encode a map of the space in which the animal navigates, and human studies similarly point to an important role of the hippocampus in building maps of the world—spatial as well as conceptual. In a famous experiment, a small number of London cab drivers' brains were compared to brains of the average Londoner; the researchers observed that one part of the hippocampus seemed to be larger in the cab drivers (though whether cab driving was the cause or the effect of such enlargement is not clear).

The roles of the hippocampus in episodic memory and spatial representation are likely closely linked. After all, where you are and where you've been are important kinds of autobiographical events that we would expect the hippocampus to store. Moreover, evidence indicates that as we prospect about the future (such as planning what path we will take on a road trip or what we will do when we arrive at the beach), we draw on hippocampal mechanisms to simulate such imagined events. In this way, the hippocampus—interacting with prefrontal cortex and other structures—not only enables us to travel back in time, bringing details from the past forward to inform the present, but also to project us forward in time, constructing possible futures that inform our thoughts and behaviors when we eventually land in the future. These processes are powerful and confer many benefits, but also can create costs, such as when we mistakenly believe that an imagined event—which ends up stored in memory just like true events—was actually experienced or distorts our memory of what actually was an experienced event.

Amygdala

One of the limbic structures to which the hippocampus is most richly connected is the *amygdala*, an almond-shaped structure that derives its name from the Greek word for almond. The amygdala is a collection of neurons within the rostral (front) tip of the medial temporal lobe, situated anterior to the hippocampus. Generally speaking, the amygdala is a kind of neural alarm system, tagging experiences as important across a wide range of evolutionary salience, ranging from "Hey, there's some food" to "Hey, someone's pointing a gun at me" to "Hey, that attractive person just smiled at me" to "Hey, that person just shoplifted." Given its role as the brain's central alarm, one of the amygdala's many significant jobs is to mediate the relationship between emotion and memory, a relationship that can be devilishly complex.

A deeply emotional experience can be so powerful that we never forget it, but also so emotional that we continue to overrespond to it. It will take you quite a long time to go back to that alley where you were robbed, but eventually we often are able to get over the panic (even if not the memory). Indeed, returning to the alley and creating new, more positive or at least neutral memories is an effective element of treating such anxiety. The existence of these newer memories can interfere with the retrieval of the original negative memory, decreasing the likelihood that it will come to mind—in essence, by building new positive or neutral memories that become dominant, we are less likely to remember the older memory. As a consequence, there is an uncoupling of the association of one set of facts (the alley) from another unpleasant set of facts (the robbery), not because the association is lost from memory but because other associations with the alley become more dominant. Active research is also exploring additional ways to regulate memory, such as using control regions in the cortex, especially parts of the prefrontal cortex (PFC) described in Chapter 3, to exert a kind of "top-down" suppression of the amygdala or the hippocampus. Deficiencies in the ability to block access to difficult memories or to suppress the amygdala are thought to contribute to some anxiety disorders, including PTSD.

Deeply emotional experiences might be more strongly stored in memory and can give rise to a strong sense of reliving the event when remembering. It is now thought that this strong sense of reliving is due, at least in part, to the reactivation of amygdala responses at the time of remembering; we subjectively experience such reactivation of emotion at the time of retrieval as a re-experiencing of the event, and we interpret it as compelling evidence that our memory is strong and accurate. However, it is important to understand that this does not mean such memories are not subject to the normal workings of memory. Indeed, while we are often highly confident in such memories—sometimes referring to them as "flashbulb" memories that are seared in our minds and asserting that we are certain we will never forget them—research indicates that they are also impacted by reconstructive processes at the time of retrieval. As a consequence, they are just as likely to be distorted over time, with each act of remembering, leading us to sometimes express high confidence in a memory that is inaccurate or false.

It is also notable that deeply emotional experiences can sometimes inhibit, rather than overstimulate, our memories. At the extreme, stress can interfere with the hippocampus's ability to lay down and consolidate memories, and, as mentioned previously, moderate to high levels of stress, while facilitating memory for certain event features, can lead to ineffective encoding of other event features. The amygdala, again, seems to be at the center of these phenomena, presumably sending such strong alarm signals to the hippocampus that those signals can sometimes suppress either the laying down of the memories or their consolidation. The amygdala can also send signals to brain regions involved in the perception of an event and thus impact which aspects of the event are attended to and stored in memory (e.g., the gun) at the cost of attending to and encoding other aspects (e.g., the perpetrator's face or clothing).

Legal fact-finders may have to decide questions such as whether a victim's fear during an armed robbery enhanced or inhibited his memory for details of the event. Or they may have to determine how to weigh a witness's statement of high confidence in her memory against other evidence in the case that may conflict with the memory. Such legally relevant questions, whose answers are today really unknown (at least at the level of an individual brain and an individual memory), are questions about the complex dance between the hippocampus, the amygdala, the cingulate cortex, the insula, and various portions of PFC and other cortical areas.

Hypothalamus and Pituitary Gland

Hypothalamus means below the thalamus, and that's just where it is, below (ventral to) the thalamus and right on top of the pituitary gland. As with the thalamus, the hypothalamus is richly connected to the brainstem. All vertebrates have a hypothalamus, and its primary function seems to be to regulate internal body states—a function biologists call *homeostasis*. The hypothalamus accomplishes homeostasis by regulating the body's internal states and related emotions, including temperature, hunger, thirst, sex drive, fatigue, sleep, and circadian rhythm. This regulation is done through neural connections between the hypothalamus on the one hand, and the autonomic nervous and endocrine systems on the other hand. Many effects of stress are mediated through the hypothalamus.

The secretion of hormones is governed largely through the *pituitary gland*, a structure also located near the very base of the brain. The pituitary gland is both a gland and a brain structure. It releases a handful of its own hormones, including human growth hormone from its anterior segment and an important substance we will discuss later called oxytocin from its posterior segment. Additionally, it influences the release of hormones by other glands. Because of this dual ability to directly and indirectly regulate hormone secretions, neuroscientists sometimes call the pituitary gland the "master gland."

BASAL GANGLIA

A second functional grouping of interior structures is called the *basal ganglia*. "Basal," as we now know, means below, and "ganglia" simply means a dense collection of neurons. The basal ganglia consist of several dense collections of neurons found below the cortex, each with a descriptive name (Figure 4.2). We will introduce just two of them: the *striatum* and the *substantia nigra*. Generally, the circuitry of the basal ganglia seems dedicated to three interrelated tasks: voluntary movement, habituation, and motivation. Disorders of the basal ganglia, whether by stroke, atrophy, or inherited genes, can cause a host of neurological problems, including Parkinson's and Huntington's diseases. Besides problems with movement, basal ganglia patients can exhibit obsessive compulsive disorder and addiction, each of which can of course entail a variety of legal issues.

Striatum

The *striatum* is a large structure forming the lateral wall of the major ventricle in the brain. It is named after its striped appearance, which is caused by streaks of myelinated axons passing through the collection of neurons on their way to the spinal cord. As noted previously, the striatum receives input from the cerebral cortex and sends signals along two major pathways: one that will encourage an action and another that will discourage the action. The basal ganglia influence both thought and emotion as well as action. Patients with Parkinson's disease who are slowed in moving can also be slowed in thinking.

The striatum is functionally and structurally divided into dorsal and ventral portions. The dorsal striatum contributes to the planning, production, and inhibition of movements and to learning how to produce skilled movements. Scientists summarize the function of the dorsal striatum in terms of learning habits and acquiring motor skills. When you perform an automatic but highly skilled movement, such as driving your car, with no conscious memory of doing so, your dorsal striatum can be thanked. The fact that skilled actions can be performed automatically and unconsciously creates interesting legal questions when responsibility for the action becomes an issue. When the law confronts these questions of a defendant as "unconscious actor," he may be held less responsible because he acted with a lesser state of mind, like reckless and negligent, or perhaps he will not be held responsible at all via doctrines of involuntariness.

The ventral striatum is primarily involved with the risk-reward circuit discussed in Chapter 3. It functions at the crossroads of neural networks contributing to our sense of reward, our motivation, and the weighing of options based on expected value.

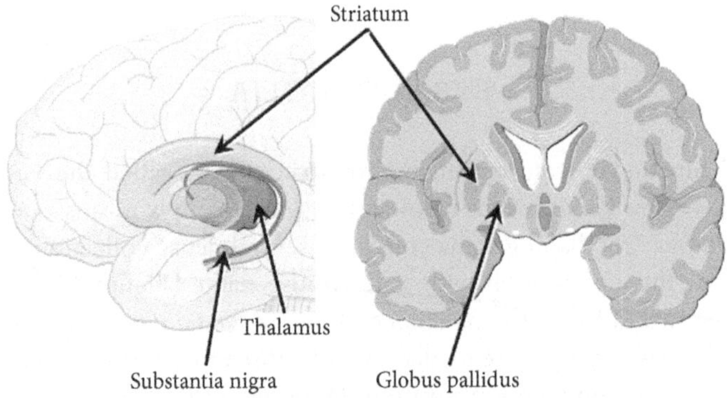

FIGURE 4.2 The thalamus and some structures of the basal ganglia.

The roles of dorsal striatum in building habits and ventral striatum in evaluating rewards can be distorted by addictive drugs and activities. For example, neurons in the striatum are sensitive to opioid drugs, and many other psychotropic drugs have indirect influences on the basal ganglia. Scientists have associated severe addiction with circuit changes in the striatum. In both the dorsal and ventral striatum, the knife's edge balance between acting and not acting, thinking and not thinking, feeling and not feeling is tuned by an important input to the striatum, described next.

Substantia Nigra

Named for its black appearance, the *substantia nigra* is part of the basal ganglia and is located in the brainstem. It has many functions, but we will emphasize one major contribution: the delivery of the neurotransmitter dopamine to the striatum and other brain areas. With the appropriate level of dopamine, the striatum will effectively balance the pros and cons of contemplated actions and is thus a critical piece of the brain's decision-making machinery. Parkinson's disease is caused by the death of dopamine neurons in the substantia nigra. The movement and cognitive symptoms of the disease become evident when the amount of dopamine provided to the striatum decreases so much that the balance of doing and not doing cannot be maintained. This, too, may raise challenges for legal notions of responsibility. Have patients with Parkinson's disease acted "intentionally," or even "voluntarily," if their judgments have been severely compromised by dopamine imbalance caused by damage to the substantia nigra?

The critical role of the substantia nigra in delivering dopamine to the striatum and elsewhere in the brain brings us now to how neurons work, and how their working depends on dopamine and other neurotransmitters.

5

HOW NEURONS WORK

> A group of high school football players brought design defect and failure-to-warn claims against helmet-maker Ridell, Inc., claiming that Ridell's negligence caused them to suffer mild traumatic brain injuries incurred while they were practicing and playing wearing Ridell helmets. Ridell moved for summary judgment, in part on the ground that the opinion of the plaintiffs' sole causation expert was insufficient to show causation as to either claim. That opinion stated only that mild TBI could be caused from the impacts endured during football, but failed to connect any of the alleged design defects to any of the plaintiffs' injuries. The trial court granted the motion for summary judgment as to the design claim, but not as to the failure-to-warn claim.
>
> *Adams v. BRG Sports, Inc., Case No. 17 C 8544 (N.D. Ill., April 17, 2021).*

INTRODUCTION

All of the functional brain areas and structures discussed in the prior chapters are built from neurons—brain cells that communicate with each other through complex but well-understood electrical and chemical processes. The first thing to know about neurons is that they are *excitable,* which means that their electrical state can be excited (on) or not (off). Through this excitability, neurons interact by receiving and delivering signals. Some of these signals are received from the senses, and others are delivered to the muscles. Most signals influencing neurons are from other neurons.

Neurons in some parts of the nervous system interact as simply and reliably as a reflex, like the rotation of your eyes in the direction opposite the direction of rotation of your head (go ahead, look in the mirror and try it). But other circuits—especially the judgment and decision-making functions the law usually cares about—are extraordinarily complex and poorly understood.

Brain Science for Lawyers, Judges, and Policymakers. Owen D. Jones, Jeffrey D. Schall, Francis X. Shen, Morris B. Hoffman and Anthony D. Wagner, Oxford University Press. © Oxford University Press 2024.
DOI: 10.1093/oso/9780197748855.003.0005

As we saw in Chapter 2, an average adult brain contains around 86,000,000,000 neurons. If we think of brain "states" at any instant as being defined by whether each of our neurons is either firing or not firing at that instant, then we have $2^{86,000,000,000}$ possible brain states, which is more than the estimated number of particles in the known universe. On the other hand, readers who are computer savvy will notice that the storage capacity of the brain is rather unimpressive, looking just at the number of neurons. If we analogize each neuron to an on-off bit in a computer (an analogy, we will see, that is not entirely apt), that means the brain is a measly 11-gigabyte machine (1 gigabyte = 10 billion bytes = 80 billion bits). You can carry hundreds of gigabytes on the flash drive or smartphone in your pocket.

The real complexity of the brain lies not in the sheer number of its neurons, but in the extent, diversity, and flexibility of their interconnectivity. As we saw in Chapter 2, the average neuron in the cerebral cortex is connected to roughly 10,000 other neurons. But it's not just the degree of interconnectedness that accounts for the brain's complexity. What really makes the brain so complex is the nature of those connections. Unlike computers, brains are not hardwired. Neural connections are formed, dissolved, reformed, strengthened, and weakened across our lifespans through development, experience, and injury. Moreover, neurons communicate with one another by releasing one or more of dozens of different chemicals. These chemicals influence other neurons (or glands or muscles) and can even influence the neuron doing the releasing. There is thus a profoundly self-referential aspect of this complex network.

You should also know that although in this chapter we will be describing only one idealized type of neuron, in fact over 200 different types have been identified, each with unique shapes, on/off properties, and chemical signals. The following discussion focuses on the most basic characteristics of neurons that are common across all types.

We saw in Chapter 2 that neurons are single cells, and, just like most of the body's single cells, they have a single nucleus. But unlike other cells, neurons are equipped with a long structure—the axon—which allows the neuron to signal to other neurons (or muscles or glands) some distance away from the cell body. For example, the neurons in the motor cortex that make your toes flex or extend are located in the cerebral cortex near the top of your head, and their axons runs to the small of your back, where they meet other neurons' axons that carry the message all the way down to the toes.

Neurons are said to be excitable because their cell membranes (their "skins") are like tiny batteries that can conduct electrical current. We will refer to this electrical current as a *nerve impulse*. Nerve impulses are conveyed automatically along the axon. The electrical current, or signal, forms the basis of the neuron's informational capacity. Nearly all neurons receive signals from other neurons, and, depending on their strength and timing, those signals can cause the receiving neuron to change from the "off" to the "on" state, which results in a nerve impulse being conveyed along the axon to other neurons.

For example, to flex your toes (go ahead, now), neurons in the motor cortex at the top of your brain send electrical signals along axons to the lumbar spinal cord, and neurons in the spinal cord send signals from the spinal cord to the muscles in your legs and feet. Thus, axons can be very long. However, they can also be submicroscopically short, connecting with neighboring neurons.

To help the electrical current travel down its length, many axons are covered in a periodically interrupted insulating material called *myelin*, akin to how wires are covered with insulation, but with regular breaks in the covering. Different kinds of neurons have different amounts of myelin, which results in different transmission speeds. For example, there are two different kinds of neurons involved with pain transmission—one set is fast, and it gives us the sensation of sharp pain; the other is much slower and is associated with the duller throbbing kind of pain.

An important part of the brain's developmental processes involves myelination. We are born with very little myelin, add large quantities of it over time (especially through infancy but all the way through adolescence), and can then lose it in old age. Significant loss of myelin is the hallmark of many neurodegenerative autoimmune diseases, including multiple sclerosis and Guillain-Barré syndrome.

Because the myelin is white, axons in the aggregate take on a white hue. Thus, as a reminder from Chapter 3, the brain's *white matter* refers to myelinated axons. The *gray matter* is made up of all the neurons' unmyelinated cell bodies, together with the glial cells (which, you will recall from Chapter 2, provide the neurons with a scaffold, a supply of nutrients and a trash collector).

Also recall from Chapter 2 that the tips of the axons are the output end of a neuron, and the dendrites—the tree or bush-like branches sprouting from the cell body—are its receiving end. The point where a neuron's axon "contacts" a downstream neuron's dendrite is actually a small space called the *synapse* (Greek for "conjunction," as in fasten together). Neurons transmit information to one another by releasing a chemical, called a *neurotransmitter*, which crosses the synapse from the axon of the sending cell to contact the dendrite of the receiving cell (Figure 5.1).

It is hard to overstate the importance of our 100 trillion synapses because it is the communication between neurons at these synapses that facilitates all of our mental life—and disruptions in those communication circuits can lead to medical and legal

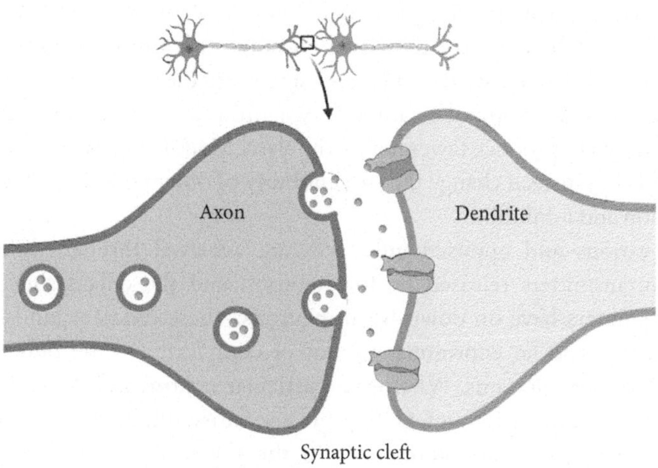

FIGURE 5.1 Communication at the synapse.

problems. The development of our brain's synaptic pathways begins in the womb and continues throughout life in response to both internal and external stimuli.

The process of brain development involves both making new neuronal connections and pruning old ones. At birth, the brain's many neurons expand their connections with one another in a process called *synaptogenesis*. It is estimated that the peak number of synapses occurs around age two to three. At that point, certain connections are further strengthened and other connections are pruned away. It is sometimes said that neurons that "fire together wire together" and that synaptic development is a "use it or lose it" process. Neither of these phrases precisely captures the complexity of brain development, but they do describe a core feature of the developing brain: neuronal connections at the synapse are very responsive to internal (e.g., immune system) and external (e.g., social interaction) stimuli. Neurodegenerative diseases can cause significant problems by destroying important synaptic connections and disrupting critical brain functions.

One legally relevant aspect of brain development is the effect of early life adversity—such as physical abuse, malnutrition, and toxins—on subsequent life outcomes. While the causal mechanisms remain under investigation, there is evidence to suggest that, on average, such early adverse experiences can raise the likelihood of abnormal brain development, onset of mental disorder, and likelihood of antisocial behavior.

While the basic contours of synaptogenesis and pruning are known, there remains debate in the literature about the extent to which *plasticity* (the ability of the brain to modify its connections) continues throughout the lifespan for different circuits and the extent to which plasticity depends on *critical periods* (the limited period in which a given brain development may occur) and *sensitive periods* (when development is more easily achieved). As we age, it becomes more difficult (though not impossible) to change some firing patterns. This is in part why so much focus is placed on development in the earliest years (and even while babies are still in the womb). Those babies' brains are creating networks that will have a great influence on how their adult brains will operate.

There are three main functional types of neurons distinguished by the three different types of influences that they have on other neurons: excitatory, inhibitory, and modulatory. Excitatory neurons send signals that cause downstream neurons to produce more nerve impulses. Inhibitory neurons send signals that cause downstream neurons to produce fewer nerve impulses. Modulatory neurons don't really send signals but instead change the susceptibility of other neurons to the influence of excitation and inhibition.

These various and opposed influences are achieved through differences in the neurotransmitters released by the neurons, and the effects those different neurotransmitters have on downstream neurons. These different kinds of signals and influences add an enormous amount of complexity to the brain's network of 86,000,000,000 neurons. Whether a particular neuron will convey a message downstream depends on its integrating the excitatory, inhibitory, and modulating messages coming into its dendrites from the thousands of upstream neurons influencing it. Current theories on cortical function hold that excitation and inhibition are maintained in careful balance, so that whether a given neuron will produce a nerve impulse is rather unpredictable.

Over 100 different neurotransmitters have been discovered to date. The synapse can be thought of as a complex and ever-changing soup of neurotransmitters, which at any moment either will or will not allow a message to continue across to the downstream neuron.

Neural signaling must be flexible so that it can react to changing circumstances in the world, body, and brain. To maintain this flexibility, neurotransmitters cannot remain in the synaptic space for too long. If a given neurotransmitter stays in the synaptic space, it will make it easier (if it's excitatory) or harder (if it's inhibitory) for that same neuron to pass its next electrical message along the network. Flexibility therefore requires that neurotransmitters be removed from the synapse once they do their job of allowing (or blocking) a signal.

This removal is accomplished through several different mechanisms. Some of the neurotransmitter molecules are absorbed back into the axon terminal for reuse. Some neurons release substances that chemically break down the neurotransmitter, inactivating it. Others deactivate neurotransmitters indirectly by releasing substances that block the neurotransmitter's ability to bind to downstream dendrites.

Neuroscientists are interested in all of these processes, and they have discovered that psychoactive drugs have their effects by facilitating or interfering with the many steps of neurotransmitter release, binding, and inactivation. Some of these drugs are mistaken by neurons for natural neurotransmitters. Substances that have the same effect as the natural neurotransmitter are called *agonists*. For example, heroin is a potent agonist for a class of naturally occurring opioid receptors. Other drugs interfere with natural neurotransmitters; these are called *antagonists*. For example, a dopamine receptor antagonist will suppress neural transmissions that depend on dopamine. This can be useful to alleviate symptoms arising from excessive dopamine.

Another class of psychoactive drugs inhibits the neurotransmitter reuptake process. You may have heard of a class of psychotropic drugs called *SSRI*, which stands for *selective serotonin reuptake inhibitor*. These drugs inhibit the reuptake of a neurotransmitter called serotonin, discussed later, leaving more in the synaptic space for a longer time and thereby increasing the serotonin's influence.

Neuromodulators—as opposed to neurotransmitters that signal directly between two neurons—affect synaptic transmission for longer duration and in more indirect ways. The brain has a number of neuromodulatory systems. Each begins in nerve cell bodies located in the brainstem and base of the brain, and they deliver their neuromodulators to many cortical areas simultaneously.

Neuromodulators work through what neuroscientists call a *second messenger system* contained in the receiving neuron's dendrites. When neuromodulators bind to those dendrites, they don't just cause excitation or inhibition. Instead, they trigger a variety of processes that amplify influence through chemical cascades. These diverse cascades modify many aspects of neuron function.

For example, they can increase or decrease the number of receptors for the direct excitatory or inhibitory neurotransmitters. Through effects like this, modulatory neurotransmitters have a broader and longer-acting range of effects than other kinds of neurotransmitters. Scientists often use the more general term "neurotransmitter" to cover both neurotransmitters and neuromodulators, and we will follow that convention. Of the hundred or so human neurotransmitters discovered to date, most are neuromodulators, including several of which you may have heard. We will now survey four of the most well known of them: dopamine, serotonin, norepinephrine, and oxytocin.

DOPAMINE

Dopamine may be the most well known of all neurotransmitters, probably because of its association with the feeling of pleasure, the fact that it was discovered in 1958 at the dawn of mass media, and its importance for the treatment of both Parkinson's disease and schizophrenia.

Dopamine is one of the ways evolution encouraged us to do important behaviors necessary for survival and reproduction, like eating and having sex. When we do (or even just anticipate doing) those things, we feel pleasure, which seems to be an effect of the release of dopamine, which then tags these events as things we may want to do again in the future. This happens because dopamine is key to the reward half of our risk-reward network, the corticostriatal pathway we discussed in Chapter 3. Some drugs, like cocaine, can change the dopamine system and other elements of the risk-reward network, leading to addiction.

Dopamine is also crucial for producing deliberate actions. A lack of dopamine is the fundamental cause of Parkinson's disease. As we saw in Chapter 2, a common and effective treatment for Parkinson's disease is a drug known as L-DOPA, which passes through the blood-brain barrier and is then converted by the brain into dopamine. Conversely, schizophrenia is associated with too much dopamine in the brain, and some of the first effective antipsychotic drugs were dopamine receptor antagonists, meaning they interfere with the ability of dopamine to bind to receptors on the dendritic side of the synapse. Dopamine is also thought to contribute to hippocampal-dependent memory, as dopamine release can be triggered by novel or unexpected events and serves as a tag that increases the likelihood that the hippocampus will consolidate the memory of the event.

SEROTONIN

Serotonin is another important neurotransmitter. Produced in specialized regions of the brainstem, serotonin contributes to many functions, from regulating sleep and wakefulness to influencing whether you feel anxious or calm. Hallucinogenic drugs like LSD work, in part, by artificially stimulating serotonin receptors. The "runner's high"—the euphoric feeling reported after vigorous exercise—was once thought to be caused primarily by a surge in serotonin, though it now appears that other neuromodulators may also be involved, including endocannabinoids (naturally occurring forms of cannabis). As with dopamine, unbalanced serotonin levels are associated with various disorders. Reduced levels of serotonin have been linked with depression, anxiety, obsessive-compulsive disorder, impulsive behavior, social phobia, and alcoholism. SSRIs increase the amount of serotonin available at synapses, which makes them useful in treating these disorders. Too much serotonin can cause schizophrenia, for which serotonin antagonists such as clozapine and trazadone have proven useful in treatment. Through a complex interplay of genetics and environment, excess serotonin has also been associated with aggression and impulsive violence.

NOREPINEPHRINE

Norepinephrine is an important neurotransmitter and hormone involved both with the nerves that run the heart and lungs, and more generally with arousal. Epinephrine is a synonym for adrenaline. The "nor" part of the word simply means that the epinephrine is acting as a neurotransmitter and has been made by neurons clustered in the brainstem. Epinephrine is also made by the adrenal gland, which is located above the kidney and which releases epinephrine directly into the bloodstream.

Norepinephrine is critical to fight-or-flight pathways running through the amygdala, and also projects to other systems of the brain, affecting attention, learning, and memory. When we see that gun being pointed at us, norepinephrine is signaling neurons in the amygdala and other parts of the fight-or-flight network. At the same time, the adrenal glands are dumping extra epinephrine into our bloodstream, increasing our heart and breathing rates, dilating our blood vessels, and sending large amounts of oxygen and glucose to our muscles, all so that we are primed to act.

Too little norepinephrine is associated with low blood pressure and depression; too much, with schizophrenia. Norepinephrine itself is sometimes injected into the bloodstream as a treatment for critically low blood pressure. The blood-brain barrier blocks its uptake in the brain, so other indirect methods are used to alter the brain's levels of norepinephrine, including the well-known drug Ritalin, which inhibits the reuptake of norepinephrine and of dopamine.

OXYTOCIN

The last neurotransmitter we will discuss is *oxytocin*. It is made primarily in the hypothalamus and released through the pituitary gland into the bloodstream. All mammals have oxytocin because one of its primary functions is to stimulate lactation.

Oxytocin is also critical to a wide variety of pro-social emotional states we might generally label as "trust" or "cooperation." Increased levels of oxytocin are associated with things like pair-bonding, socialization, grooming, and empathy. Experimental subjects with higher oxytocin levels are more likely to trust each other.

Importantly, the relationship of oxytocin and trust is a two-way street. Trusting someone (or getting groomed or massaged by them, which, when you think about it, is a fundamental kind of trust) causes oxytocin levels to increase in the blood stream. Even being trusted by someone can increase oxytocin. Evolutionary biologists have surmised that oxytocin was critical to our human ancestors because it acted as a kind of glue that allowed us to trust each other enough to live in large groups.

***

The importance of synaptic connections, and neurotransmitters' roles in making those connections, is hard to overstate. According to one neuroscientist, we are "synaptic selves." Everything we think and do requires communication between cells at these synapses.

We hope you can see from this brief summary of how neurons work and influence each other that the brain is substantially more complex than an 11-gigabyte computer. In fact, neuroscientists estimate that the brain's "capacity," continuing the imperfect computer analogy, ranges somewhere between a terabyte (1,000 gigabytes) and a petabyte (1,000,000 gigabytes). The interaction between neurons, the neurotransmitters and neuromodulators they release, and the effects such release have on the neuron's own receptivity, both directly and through the second messenger system, are the self-referential processes by which brains configure themselves into virtually uncountable numbers of combinations with astonishing speed. Somehow, in ways that are still largely unknown, high-order functions like learning, feeling, thinking, judging, and deciding are accomplished through these complex network processes.

While we don't know exactly how these processes are produced by brain cells, researchers and clinicians are making progress in unraveling brain mysteries through the use of new technologies. In the next chapter, we introduce the tools and methods that researchers and clinicians use to study human brain structure.

6

TECHNOLOGIES THAT REVEAL BRAIN STRUCTURES

Sook Li was 84 when she wrote a will that left $1,000 each to her two daughters, and the balance of her substantial estate, which included the family home in which the entire extended family had resided, to her son. After she died, her daughters contested the will, claiming that their late mother lacked testamentary capacity because of her Parkinson's disease, a condition confirmed by testimony from the mother's neurologist and psychiatrist. The probate court found the daughters had failed to overcome the presumption of capacity. Under New York law, a testator has the capacity to execute a will if he or she "understands in a general way the nature and extent of his or her property being disposed and knows the natural objects of his or her bounty." The trial court found, on summary judgment, that the mere diagnosis of Parkinson's disease, with no other evidence of specific cognitive deficits that could impinge on any of the elements of testamentary capacity, was insufficient to overcome the presumption. That conclusion was affirmed on appeal.

In re Sook Li, 72 Misc. 3d 988, 151 N.Y.S.3d 845 (N.Y. Surr. Ct. 2021).

INTRODUCTION

The previous chapters reviewed the basics of what is currently known about how the human brain works. In this chapter we turn to the methods and tools scientists used to uncover this information. Historically, to study brain structure required dissection of a dead animal or dead human. Brain structure was also examined when the living brain was exposed by grisly battle wounds, other head trauma, or neurosurgery.

Even when scientists could examine the general structure of the human brain, their observations lacked many details. The brain has the color and texture of

Brain Science for Lawyers, Judges, and Policymakers. Owen D. Jones, Jeffrey D. Schall, Francis X. Shen, Morris B. Hoffman and Anthony D. Wagner, Oxford University Press. © Oxford University Press 2024.
DOI: 10.1093/oso/9780197748855.003.0006

congealed oatmeal, and it was difficult to distinguish the constituent parts of this mushy substance. In the nineteenth century, scientists learned how to make very thin slices of the brain and to visualize different aspects of its structure by exposing the slices to a variety of chemicals, like the dyes used for clothing fibers, that would stain neurons, glia, or myelin. Brain-staining revealed unexpected structure in different parts of those slices. The brain is not an undifferentiated mass, but has very definite and particular structures. Some of those structures could be seen with the naked eye, but when the stained slices were viewed under a microscope, more elaborate details about the tissue of the brain and the structure of neurons became evident.

Staining was a major methodological advance, but this kind of anatomical study is still limited to dead nervous systems. Learning more about the structures of living human brains would have to wait until the twentieth century and the development of technologies that could detect variations in brain tissue without cutting open the skull. In this chapter we will discuss four of those noninvasive technologies. Three will be familiar to most readers: x-ray, computed axial tomography (CAT, or just CT), and structural magnetic resonance imaging (MRI). The fourth, diffusion tensor imaging (DTI), which is a form of MRI, may be less well known. The first three technologies are used on other parts of the body as well as the brain, but DTI is specialized for the brain.

A cautionary note: each of these methods for detecting brain structures has inherent limitations, including limits on spatial, contrast, and temporal resolution, and some are better than others at imaging the soft tissue of the brain. An x-ray can resolve structures as thin as a strand of hair, but is not as effective at imaging soft tissue. Even more importantly, there are limits on the inferences that scientists can draw from structural images. Although the basic plan of the brain is quite consistent across the population, the finer details of brain structure still vary significantly, not only between individuals' brains at a given time but also within an individual's brain through time. In Chapter 9, we will discuss these limitations, and the impact they have on how experiments are designed and what those experiments can and cannot show; the same limits, of course, apply to the use of these methods in legal proceedings.

We must highlight another cautionary note about what brain images are and are not. The brain "images" you will encounter medically or forensically are not simple photographs. They do not duplicate what our eyes would see if only that troublesome skull were transparent and we could probe someone's brain without doing any damage. Instead, they are representations of the physical effects that a brain is having on various beams or waves thrown at it. An x-ray, for example, records how much of the radiation bounces off of, is scattered by, or passes right through the skin, skull, and brain.

Of course, in this sense the images we see with our eyes are also not exactly "images" either. Our eyes are recording the effects that objects have in scattering ordinary light in the visual range of the spectrum. Nevertheless, the important point is that the "visualizing" technologies we discuss in this chapter change the form of the visualization from our common experience of seeing with our eyes into very different forms. Although that is obvious in the case, say, of x-rays—anyone comparing an x-ray to a photograph of an actual brain can see the difference—it may be less obvious when we get to more recently developed technologies, such as structural MRI and DTI. We will also see a version of this problem in the next chapter when we get to some of the technologies that "visualize" brain function, such as functional MRI (fMRI). They are typically not measuring, let alone visualizing, neural responses that have real (absolute) units, but laypeople (and some careless neuroscientists) sometimes describe a functional image as showing the brain "lighting up." If any of your experts use such language, you might consider hiring someone else.

X-RAY

In 1895, the German physicist Wilhelm Röntgen noticed that when he shined recently discovered cathode rays onto a distant wall, he saw a glow that seemed to be coming from inside the wall. He proposed that the glow was the result of a previously undiscovered kind of radiation, later dubbed the *x-ray*, and spent just a few weeks of intense experimentation to perfect the technique. To illustrate his findings, he published a paper containing an image of the bones in his wife's hand. Röntgen won the 1901 Nobel Prize for Physics.

X-rays are a kind of radiation which, like all radiation, gets absorbed to varying degrees depending on the density of the material through which it is passing. X-rays are produced by causing electrons to be knocked out of their orbits. This can be done in several different ways, including the way Röntgen used—heating up a negatively charged rod (cathode, thus the synonym "cathode rays") in a vacuum and letting its released electrons collide at high velocity with a metal target.

Generally, when x-rays strike an object they are reflected more by denser objects and absorbed by less dense ones. Thus, very dense material, like bone, reflects a greater portion of the x-rays than softer material like skin. This is how Mrs. Röntgen's finger bones appeared bright and the overlaying tissue almost not at all.

The good news about x-rays is that they have very high spatial resolution (about 0.1 mm), meaning that they can "see" things as small as the width of a strand of hair. But the bad news is that they lack contrast. They are terrific at imaging bone and other high-density materials, but below a certain density everything else just looks like a mass of gray. While a bit of an exaggeration, it is as if we took our high-definition color TV and reprogrammed it to show just two colors: white for every color above a certain brightness, and gray for everything else. The baseball players' white uniforms, the ball, and the bases would all be clear as ever, but everything else would be a mass of gray.

As a result of these limitations, ordinary x-rays are spectacular at showing bones and a few other high-density structures, but terrible at showing softer tissues. If we had bony skin and soft insides (like insects and other animals with exoskeletons), ordinary x-rays would be virtually useless. And of course, there is a place on our body with a bony outside and soft inside—our heads. Like the baseball game reprogrammed on our high-definition TV, ordinary brain x-rays show the skull as bright white and everything inside the brain as an undifferentiated mass of gray.

This lack of contrast can be improved by injecting subjects with dyes that reflect more x-rays and that are transported into blood vessels and different tissues. In this way, x-rays can be used to differentiate some soft tissues, including brain tissue and blood vessels. X-rays with high-density contrast are commonly used to detect cysts or tumors in the brain.

As you know, an x-ray typically refers to a single image (a "still"). But the same technology can, with a few tweaks, be used to dynamically capture changes in brain structure over time. *Fluoroscopy* refers to a moving picture version of a series of x-ray stills over time. As with x-rays, fluoroscopy has high spatial resolution and poor contrast resolution but good timing (temporal) resolution. That is, with added contrast materials, fluoroscopes can show soft tissues in real time—such as the heart as it actually beats or the tongue as a person speaks. Like x-rays, fluoroscopes are two-dimensional, but like all movies, they give the illusion of movement in three dimensions. Today, fluoroscope images are capable of many spatial and other kinds of dimensional manipulations, making them more similar to CAT scans (discussed later) than ordinary x-rays. By the way, many modern airport body scanners are low radiation fluoroscopes.

COMPUTED AXIAL TOMOGRAPHY

Computed axial tomography (*CAT*, or *CT*) uses a series of two-dimensional x-rays, taken around a circle from many regularly spaced angles, to compute three-dimensional shapes. The math is complicated, but the idea is simple. Imagine you were in charge of making a sculpture that accurately depicted several objects in a room. You could take photographs of the objects (two-dimensional representations) from many different perspectives, and if you took enough photographs from enough perspectives, you could reconstruct the three-dimensional room and the objects in it. That's what CAT scans do. The typical resolution of CAT scans (combining spatial and contrast resolutions) is about 0.5 mm, two-thirds the thickness of a credit card.

As with x-rays, bones on a CAT scan image appear white, and with sufficient contrast different tissues show different shades of gray depending on their density. But unlike x-rays or even ordinary fluoroscopes, the additional spatial information, coupled with sophisticated computer programs, allows the two-dimensional x-rays to be accumulated into a three-dimensional image. The three-dimensional image is usually represented by a series of two dimensional "slices" or "sections" taken at different depths (Figure 6.1).

CAT was developed in the early 1970s and—despite some potential long-term side effects from repeated exposure to x-rays—quickly became the standard of care for the detection and diagnosis of many soft tissue injuries, including brain damage. CAT is used routinely in emergency rooms when a patient arrives with a potential traumatic brain injury.

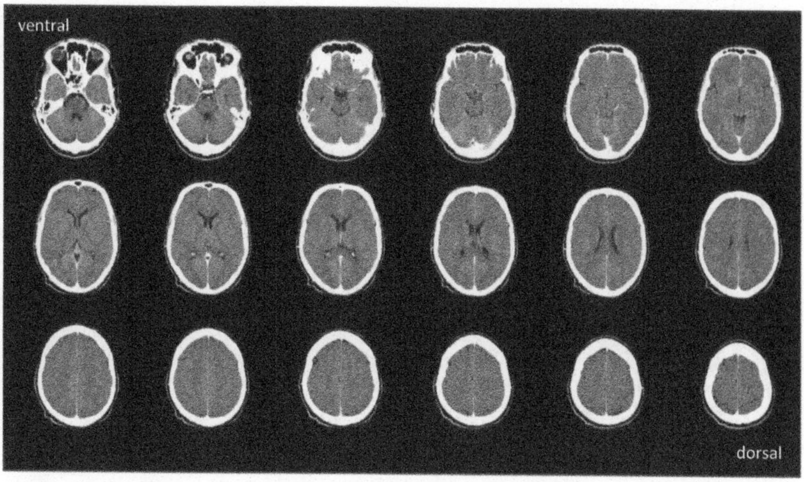

FIGURE 6.1 CAT scans of human brain in horizontal section from ventral to dorsal.

STRUCTURAL MAGNETIC RESONANCE IMAGING

Magnetic resonance imaging (*MRI*) takes advantage of the magnetic characteristics of the molecules, and their atomic constituents, that make up our bodies. MRI leverages the properties of the hydrogen atoms in the brain, which act like tiny magnets. An MRI scanner has a large and powerful tube-shaped magnet. When a subject is placed into the tube, the magnet aligns the axes of the hydrogen atoms (technically, their protons) in the subject's tissue along the large magnet's field.

Once the hydrogen atoms are aligned, other electromagnets create radiofrequency pulses to temporarily knock the hydrogen atoms off their currently aligned axes, causing them to spin like tops knocked off an upright orientation. Like a spinning top naturally recovers from a wobble, the hydrogen atoms realign with the large magnet's field (and with each other). As they recover from the electromagnetic wobble, they emit radio waves that are detected by sensors placed around the object being imaged. The strength of the radio waves will vary with the molecular environment in which the hydrogen atoms are spinning (because the environment impacts the speed with which the hydrogen atoms realign with the large magnet's field or with each other). For example, hydrogen atoms spinning in gray matter realign at a different rate than those spinning in white matter.

MRI can distinguish between different kinds of soft tissues, including brain tissues, at spatial resolutions of around 1 millimeter—a little thicker than a credit card. As with CAT, the scanner's software builds a three-dimensional model of the object being imaged, such as the subject's brain, divided into small three-dimensional boxes called *voxels* (volumetric pixels). During the image reconstruction process, each voxel is populated with a single measurement representing the radio frequency signal coming from all the hydrogen atoms in that voxel that were knocked off their forced axes. When we view a magnetic resonance "image," what we are typically seeing is a single two-dimensional slice from the three-dimensional data set, much as with CAT. The signal intensities of the different voxels are assigned different

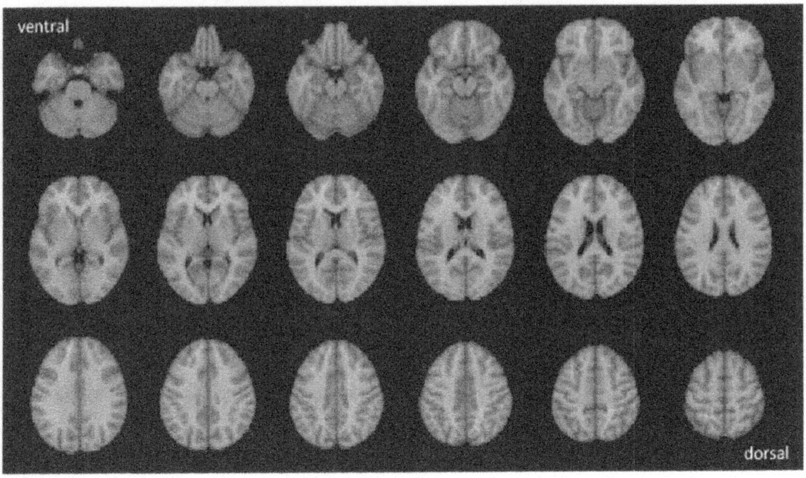

FIGURE 6.2 Structural MRI scans of human brain in horizontal section from ventral to dorsal.
Source: Stanford Memory Lab, courtesy Alexandra Trelle, PhD.

colors on a scale so they can be visualized—for structural MRI, the scale typically ranges from white to black with different shades of gray in between (Figure 6.2).

Structural MRI was first used on humans in the 1970s. Because of its high resolution and because, unlike CAT, it involves neither x-ray radiation nor the injection of any contrast dyes (for most uses), MRI quickly became a widely accepted clinical tool for aiding in the diagnosis, treatment, and understanding of soft tissue injuries and diseases. In professional sports, MRI has become a ubiquitous part of athletic medicine, with fans nervously waiting to learn the results of their favorite athlete's MRI after an injury.

MRI is especially useful when imaging brain structure. Because white and gray matter have significantly different densities and composition, MRI is very good at distinguishing between these two types of brain material, not to mention the different kinds of brain structures below the cortex that we saw in Chapter 4, and some of the fine details within those structures. MRI can also be used to measure other relevant properties of brain tissue, such as its iron density or the concentration of neuromelanin. Measurements of properties like these can vary across specific regions as a function of age and certain diseases, and can distinguish tumors from healthy tissue.

But there are some practical drawbacks to MRI. Standard scanners, and their supporting equipment, are room-sized, expensive to buy and maintain, and can be complicated to use. MRI depends on continuously active superconducting electromagnets, which are ordinarily cooled by liquid helium. Also, some scans can take as long as 30 minutes, the pulsing magnets are very loud, and the whole process can leave some subjects anxious and claustrophobic. Because the signals used to create the images are measured over time, even the smallest movements by a subject or patient inside of the scanner can cause blurring and other artifacts in the images, invalidating the results. Although new technology is being developed, at present MRI cannot be used to measure brain properties while the rest of the body is in motion. There are also restrictions on who can be scanned. Because of the very powerful magnets, subjects with ferromagnetic metal in their bodies—including certain joint replacements, pacemakers, cochlear implants, as well as eye shadow and tattoos and even machinists who have accumulated small metal shavings in their skin—cannot safely be placed inside MRI machines.

By the way, we will be referring in the next chapter to the *functional* MRI technique, which uses MRI technology to learn about brain function (rather than brain structure). The fact that that technique is commonly referred to as "fMRI" (with the "f" lowercase by convention) may cause you to wonder why *structural* MRI, discussed in this chapter, isn't correspondingly referred to as "sMRI." The answer is: it typically just isn't, probably because the use of MRI for structural purposes predated its use for functional purposes. So, if your orthopedic surgeon orders an "MRI" of your bad knee or your neurologist an "MRI" of your brain, these will probably be *structural* MRIs.

Typically, to get an MRI brain scan, you have to go to a hospital, an imaging clinic, or perhaps a scientific research facility. However, this may eventually change, as cheaper, more portable MRI systems have been built recently based on new advances in engineering, physics, and artificial intelligence. Clinical-grade magnetic resonance images (equivalent to those typically generated by MRI) may soon be produced from machines that sit in a regular room, plugged into a standard 120-volt outlet, without an elaborate helium cooling system. For example, high-quality magnetic resonance images can be produced using "ultra-low field" systems with a smaller, less powerful magnet combined with advanced techniques to extract signals from noisy data. A low field-strength structural MRI scanner is currently in clinical use at the bedside.

Mobile neuroimaging raises tantalizing possibilities. As a direct-to-consumer technology, some business plans envision a brain scanner in every pharmacy. Could brain scanners also be located in police stations, prisons, or courtrooms? Mobile neuroimaging technologies raise unique ethical and legal questions because existing recommendations have assumed that this equipment would be located within a medical or research facility and have not yet considered their use in a highly mobile context and as a potential direct-to-consumer service.

DIFFUSION TENSOR IMAGING

Diffusion tensor imaging (*DTI*) uses the very same scanning equipment as MRI, but is programmed to be optimized to detect molecules that are moving in space—a process known as diffusion. As you now know, the axons of neurons are long tubes, sometimes wrapped in myelin; the brain's wiring consists of bundles of myelinated axons that connect one region with others. As the hose in your yard restricts the flow of water, so the flow of substances in the brain, including water, is restricted by myelinated axons. By tracing the directions of water's diffusion, scientists can use DTI to connect the dots and trace a bundle of axons from one end to the other in

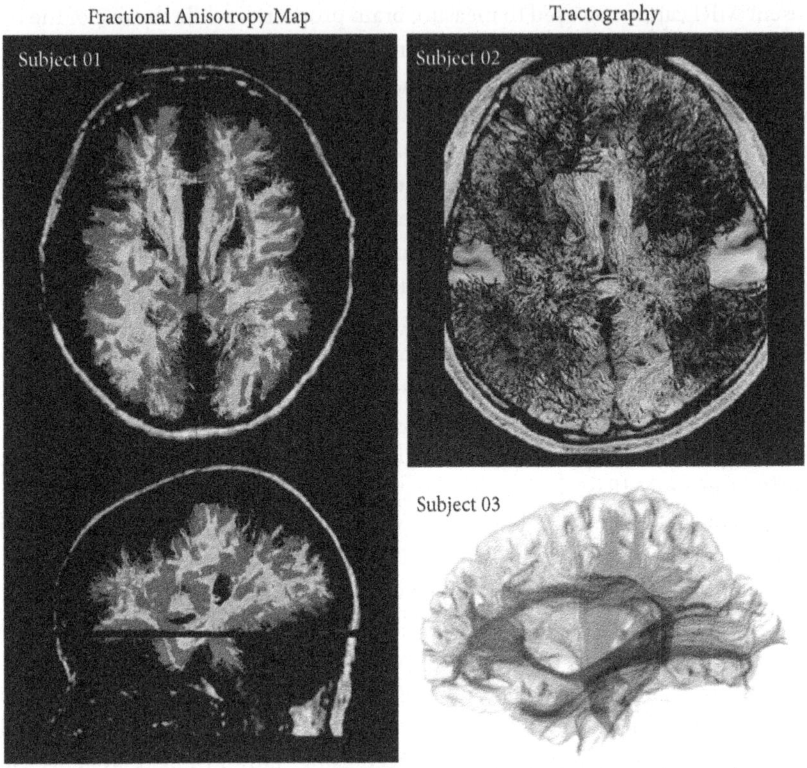

FIGURE 6.3 DTI scans of human brain in horizontal (top) and sagittal (bottom) perspectives, and showing fractional anisotropy (left) and tractography (right). *Source:* Subject 01: Stanford Memory Lab, courtesy Subbulakshmi S, PhD. Subject 02: Adapted from Pestilli et al., "Evaluation and statistical inference for human connectomes," Nat Methods, (10)11, Figure 5a, 2014. Copyright © 2014, Springer Nature America, Inc. Subject 03: Adapted from Yeatman et al., "A browser-based tool for visualization and analysis of diffusion MRI data," Nature Communications, 9, (940), Figure 6, 2018. Copyright © 2018, The Author(s).

the brain (Figure 6.3). This figure shows two different types of analyses of DTI data. Fractional anisotropy, on the left, portrays for each voxel the extent to which there is a clear direction of diffusion. Tractography, on the right, connects the dots into a connectivity map.

By the way, the beautiful colors in Figure 6.3 are not part of the original DTI images. They were added by the researcher to help visually demonstrate the different patterns of detected connectedness, a technique that we will see in the next chapter and that is also employed with PET and functional MRI.

Researchers are developing ever more complex algorithms to trace the orientation and termination of axon bundles, but the effectiveness of these new techniques remains debated. DTI offers a more modest measure of the amount of diffusion in bundles of axons, still allowing increasingly sophisticated inferences about brain network structure and function. In recent years, state and federal courts have had to rule on the admissibility of DTI for proving brain injury, and advocates in juvenile justice have used DTI to bolster claims about the developing brain and culpability.

Technologies like DTI are especially useful in studying how brains develop over time. They are an important tool for neuroscientists trying to learn how the brain develops from birth throughout adolescence and into old age, a process that touches on many aspects of the law, from rules about how old someone must be to be held responsible for a crime or to enter into a binding contract, to whether a demented testator's will should be invalidated. These connectivity technologies may also pay clinical dividends, as they shed light on the interconnected circuitry of brain diseases and disorders.

***

Having surveyed the common techniques for learning about the structure of brains inside living subjects and patients, we turn in the next chapter to survey the common techniques for learning about how a person's brain is actually functioning.

7

TECHNOLOGIES THAT REVEAL BRAIN FUNCTIONS

Thirty-two-year-old Erik Huseth pleaded guilty to possession of child pornography, admitting that he had more than 12,000 photographs and videos of child pornography, including depictions of infants and toddlers in sexual acts with adults, some suggesting sadistic or masochistic conduct. By pleading guilty, Huseth also admitted that he was able to form the culpable mental state required by the federal child pornography statute (knowingly). But at sentencing, in arguing for a downward departure from the eight to ten years of prison called for by the guidelines, Huseth's lawyer argued that his client's autism spectrum disorder (ASD) prevented him from fully appreciating the wrongfulness of the conduct. A psychologist and neuropsychologist each testified that Huseth had the social communication skills of an average eight-year-old, and that his inability to read the facial expressions and emotional states of the victims interfered with his ability to appreciate that they were being harmed. Experts called by the prosecution concurred in the ASD diagnosis, but disagreed with the defense experts' assessment of the degree of social impairment caused by the condition. They pointed out that Huseth has a high IQ and good vocabulary, attended college, and could drive a car. The sentencing judge was persuaded by the defense experts, and added that she was concerned about Huseth facing bullying and physical injuries in prison. She sentenced Huseth to probation with therapeutic conditions.

United States v. Huseth, 2021WL245248 (D. Kan., October 22, 2021).

INTRODUCTION

Discovering that the brain is made of different structures is one thing. Understanding what those structures actually do is a very different thing. Measuring brain

Brain Science for Lawyers, Judges, and Policymakers. Owen D. Jones, Jeffrey D. Schall, Francis X. Shen, Morris B. Hoffman and Anthony D. Wagner, Oxford University Press. © Oxford University Press 2024.
DOI: 10.1093/oso/9780197748855.003.0007

function is a lot more difficult than measuring brain structure, because functional measurements must be made when brains are engaged in distinct perceptions, emotions, memories, intentions, and actions. So even if the measurement device is in perfect working order, if the participant cannot or will not cooperate, then no reliable brain function can be monitored.

Much of what we know about how the brain works was discovered in two different ways: (1) by observing how strokes or accidental brain injuries impaired the functioning of people who suffered such health events; and (2) by performing experiments with nonhuman animals. Both of these methods have significant limitations. Strokes or trauma to particular parts of the brain are unpredictable and haphazard; they rarely affect only one brain region. As a means of learning about human brains, therefore, the analysis of behavior changes after brain damage requires painstaking comparisons across many patients over many years. Also, before modern neuroimaging methods were developed, the precise regions of a human brain injured by stroke or trauma could only be confirmed on autopsy, after the patient died.

Experiments with nonhuman animals permit more comprehensive and systematic investigation by way of invasive techniques that are not ethical to perform on healthy humans. The most informative involves inserting probes into the brain that can detect the occurrence of nerve impulses. Based on information gained by such experiments, variants of this methodology are used today to treat epilepsy and Parkinson's disease. Although invasive animal experiments allow researchers to construct spectacularly detailed brain maps for some functions—for example, pinpointing areas of the cerebral cortex associated with visual perception or producing discrete kinds of body movements—they tell us less about higher order brain functions such as reasoning, and almost nothing about human activities such as language and moral decision-making.

For all of these reasons, our knowledge of higher brain functioning remained primitive and spotty, until the invention of the noninvasive functional technologies described in this chapter. We will survey three of them: (1) electroencephalography (EEG); (2) positron emission tomography (PET); and (3) functional magnetic resonance imaging (fMRI). EEG was discovered in the 1920s, PET was developed in the 1970s, and fMRI became available for brain research only in the 1990s. We will discuss how each of these methods works and the complementary information each can tell us about brain function.

As with the structural technologies we saw in Chapter 6, these functional technologies have limited spatial resolutions, which we will note as we discuss each technology, as well as the significant inferential limitations we will analyze in Chapter 9. But one important limitation critical to functional imaging bears mention now: temporal resolution. Brain structures do not typically change over the short period of time that we are investigating them with the technologies discussed in the previous chapter. But when we move from structure to function, time becomes an important consideration because function happens, and changes, over time. (For how long can you hold one thought in mind without another thought interrupting?) Technologies investigating function must therefore be fast enough to detect fast functioning, and if those technologies have inherent temporal limitations, they will not be able measure changes that occur more quickly than those temporal limitations. Think of a camera slowly panning across Loch Ness—panning more slowly than Nessie is swimming and therefore never managing to capture her image. As we discuss each functional technology in the rest of this chapter, we will mention its temporal resolution.

Because these technologies allow for the measurement of brain function in living human subjects as they are performing experimental tasks, our understanding of human brain function has exploded—so much so that our descriptions of those functions in Chapters 3 and 4 were substantially simplified summaries of what is currently known about brain function. The important point, at least for purposes of this book for legal consumers, is that these technologies are now allowing systematic research into legally relevant brain functions like forming intentions, making decisions, acting voluntarily, being intoxicated or addicted, experiencing pain, and blaming and punishing others.

ELECTROENCEPHALOGRAPHY (EEG)

We saw in Chapter 5 that neurons communicate through nerve impulses that are produced when a neuron's dendrites and cell body are depolarized by synaptic transmission from other neurons. We saw in Chapter 3 that the cerebral cortex is comprised of neurons exchanging signals with one another. When millions of such anatomically aligned and functionally polarized neurons wax and wane in their activity, an electrical current is created that is strong enough to be measured by metal contacts placed on the scalp.

The *electroencephalogram*, or "electrical brain graph," is a relatively cheap and effective way of measuring these electrical fields. Traditionally, it works by fitting subjects with an array of dozens—or today sometimes hundreds—of small, metal electrical detectors, or "contacts," placed in electrical contact with the scalp with a conductive gel or solution. When the contacts are connected to an electrical amplifier, the millionths-of-a-volt changes that are evoked by a stimulus or event (what are termed *event related potentials*) or fluctuations that occur at particular frequencies (oscillations) produced by neurons in the brain can be measured and monitored. These amplified signals can be charted on paper or, more commonly today, digitized by computer for further quantification.

One common EEG approach measures things like the size of the peaks and valleys of positive and negative electrical polarization (amplitude) and the interval between those peaks and valleys (frequency). The term "brainwave" refers to the electrical polarizations produced by populations of neurons that are oscillating at particular frequencies, waxing and waning in their activity states. To appreciate the patterns observed in the EEG, think about the small, fast ripples of a pond versus the large, slow swells of the ocean. Now imagine that the small fast ripples are riding on several different levels of larger, slower swells.

When the EEG was invented, researchers soon found that both the amplitude and frequency of these waves varied with a participant's behavioral state. Generally, as someone relaxes, the amplitude of the EEG signal increases and its frequency decreases. When alert, the amplitude of the EEG signal is smaller, and frequency higher. During sleep, EEG amplitudes and frequencies vary systematically with stages of sleep. During deep sleep, the EEG is bigger and slower. During dream sleep, coinciding with rapid eye movements, the EEG is smaller and faster, more like the awake, alert state. Comatose patients have lower, slower EEG, and brain-dead patients have effectively no EEG. In another extreme case, patients experiencing epileptic seizures exhibit different patterns of highly synchronized, rapid, and large oscillations of EEG.

The variation in the oscillation frequency of EEG voltage polarizations can be analyzed conveniently by characterizing the amplitude of EEG in different ranges of frequencies. You can think of this like notes on a piano. If you hit middle C, you will hear a note with a frequency of 261.6 cycles per second (or hertz, Hz). If you hit the second key up from middle C (E), you will hear a note with a frequency of 293.7 Hz, and the second key down from middle C (A) produces a note with a frequency of 233.1 Hz. If you hit all three keys together, you will produce a chord (A minor) that combines all three frequencies.

The EEG signal can be considered a very complicated chord comprised of many different frequencies contributing different amplitudes. This complicated content of the EEG may be mathematically broken down into simpler wave components of different frequencies. Neuroscientists customarily use five ranges of frequencies, which have been labeled using the Greek alphabet. You may have heard the names given to some of these "brainwaves"—delta, theta, alpha, beta, and gamma (ordered from lowest frequency to highest). The complex electrical song emanating from the brain can be broken down into combinations of these five notes, and then measured and compared across different functions.

If you've had or seen an EEG in the distant past, you may remember the device printing out its results on a long sheet of paper. Those days are long gone. Today, EEG measurements are recorded directly by computers, which can store, analyze, and reorganize the data. And "wearable EEG" devices—which use low-power wireless collection electronics as well as "dry" contacts that need no gel—are already on the market and hold promise for many clinical, research, and recreational applications. Patients, subjects, and consumers can wear these devices at home and at work, enabling researchers and clinicians to get massive amounts of long-term EEG data that were never available before.

Portable EEG devices are also allowing researchers to investigate the neural aspects of group dynamics—what our brains are doing when we come together in a group (like a jury). There is a rich psychological literature about group dynamics, but never before has the technology permitted researchers to measure many brains simultaneously while those brains are actually involved in group decision-making. Stay tuned for those discoveries.

Versions of these portable devices, together with feedback technology and training, are also allowing paralyzed patients to move prosthetic devices and pilots to move aircraft just by thinking. Even game makers are getting into the action, marketing low-end versions of these devices that give players the ability to make moves in electronic games simply by thinking.

EEG has excellent temporal resolution, meaning it is an electrical indication of brain function in almost real time. But it has very poor spatial resolution,

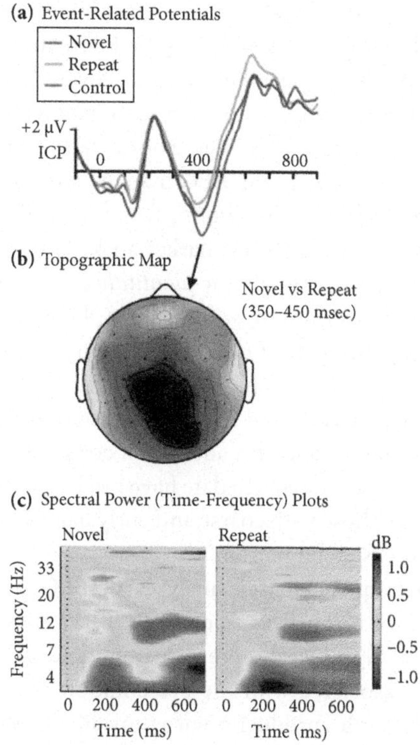

FIGURE 7.1 Three alternative analyses of EEG data.
Source: Adapted from: Race, E.A., Badre, D., & Wagner, A.D. (2010), "Multiple Forms of Learning Yield Temporally Distinct Electrophysiological Repetition Effects," *Cerebral Cortex* 20(7): 1726–1738.

because it is impossible to know where in the brain, exactly, these electrical signals originated. Most of the high-frequency signals—those most closely associated with neural impulses—are filtered out by the bones of the skull. These locations can be estimated rather coarsely by plotting the EEG signals as a function of the locations of the different electrodes placed on the scalp, which is known to offer rather limited spatial information. There are more sophisticated ways to increase EEG's spatial resolution by using structural and even functional models of the brain that enable more accurate (though still far from perfect) localization estimations. The results of these types of analyses can be displayed as colorized "maps" of the brain (Figure 7.1). Each of the images in Figure 7.1 reflects EEG data from an experiment in which participants were exposed both to stimuli they'd never seen before ("novel") and to stimuli they had seen before ("repeats"). Panel A plots EEG voltage as a function of time in both conditions. The lines (evoked responses) overlap and are statistically indistinguishable until about 400 msec (0.4 sec), at which time the brain processing of the stimuli was different in a way that caused different EEG signals. Panel B shows a topological map of the signals as they appear across the electrodes distributed across the scalp; the redder colors representing larger voltage differences. Panel C depicts the data as a function of frequency and time.

Although we call the middle figure a topological "map," as we have already said, these analyses cannot reveal exactly where in the brain any measured EEG signals were produced. Nevertheless, researchers have discovered that as long as the electrical contacts are placed on the head in the same place for each testing session, changing what subjects are doing (e.g., seeing novel versus repeat stimuli) produces reliable and predictable changes in the EEG map. As a result, EEG has become an important research tool into brain function.

In legal realms, some providers now market an EEG data analysis kit they call *QEEG*, with the Q standing, puzzlingly, for *quantitative*, even though EEG has always been quantitative. Some attorneys now have their clients undergo QEEG testing to assess whether any subtle sign of brain abnormality can be detected. We note, though, that "abnormal" EEGs will be found in about 3% of individuals without a history of neurological disease, and this classification likely heavily rests on the criteria used to define abnormality. An additional constraint on EEG research and clinical use is that most EEG systems to date have not been designed to successfully record from the scalps of those with coarse and curly hair. New work is underway to address this significant design limitation.

A complement to frequency-based analyses of EEG data is an analytic approach known as *event-related potentials*, or *ERPs*. ERPs are observed by removing the random noise in EEG to reveal more consistent and stable patterns of voltage polarizations that are associated with the presentation of a stimulus (like a beep tone or a flashed photograph), production of a movement (like pressing a button or shifting gaze) or engagement of some cognitive operation (like recognizing a photograph or planning a response that solves a puzzle). The noise removal is achieved by synchronizing (time-locking) the EEG on the event of interest and then averaging the voltages across a number of trials. The timing and magnitude of the averaged change in voltage polarizations across testing trials of that event, relative to a baseline period just prior to the event, reveals the strength of neural responses associated with sensory, cognitive, and motor processes.

To illustrate, let's say we wanted to discover what the brain's electrical field is doing when you tap your finger. Using many trials when a subject is doing nothing, the EEG averages into a background (or baseline) signal with only small, random fluctuations. Next, the EEG is averaged across all the times the subject taps a finger. An ERP related to finger-tapping is obtained by subtracting the baseline signal from the tapping signal, leaving only the finger-tapping signal. (We will see these "averaging" and "subtracting" approaches with other functional technologies, most prominently fMRI.)

Using this approach, researchers have described unique ERPs associated with many different functions, from sensory processing and body movement to cognitive tasks as complex as recognizing something familiar or unusual, forming intentions to move, and monitoring the consequences of actions. For example, in Panels A and B of Figure 7.1, researchers compared the ERPs when viewing novel stimuli to those when viewing repeated stimuli to examine the effects of novelty on the brain's response. Some investigators have even suggested that some of these ERPs can be used for lie detection, though we will see in Chapter 10 that these claims are currently quite overblown. ERPs have also been used to assess the status and possible outcomes of patients in coma, vegetative, or minimally conscious states. Note that, just like with the previously described frequency analyses of EEG data, outcomes of ERP analyses can also be rendered as spatial maps using either coarse or more sophisticated "source localization" analytic methods.

Magnetoencephalography (*MEG*) is a sister technology of EEG. It measures the magnetic fields produced by the electrical currents of aligned and temporally synchronized neurons. As with EEG, the temporal resolution of these methods is high; they can typically distinguish between responses that differ on the order of tens of milliseconds. MEG offers complementary information to that provided by EEG and also can yield higher spatial resolution than EEG, but it requires specialized, expensive equipment. Consequently, EEG is much more commonly used and therefore more likely to appear in legal contexts.

In addition to their value in research, EEG and MEG have become important clinical tools for diagnosing and monitoring a host of brain disorders, including multiple sclerosis (a disease associated with insufficient myelination), epilepsy, sleep disorders, and even when a patient is or is not brain dead. The latter question, of course, has broad legal implications.

POSITRON EMISSION TOMOGRAPHY (PET)

You have probably heard of PET scans. *PET* is an acronym for *positron emission tomography*. A *positron* is one of the elementary particles you may have skimmed over in high school physics. It is the positively charged twin of the electron and is released naturally through radioactive decay from certain kinds of atoms. Positively charged positrons naturally interact with negatively charged electrons. When a positron and electron collide, both particles are annihilated, causing the release of two gamma photons that travel in opposite directions. By using appropriate radiation detectors to encircle a brain or other body part containing low-dose radiation that has been injected into the subject, events are recorded when two opposing detectors register a "hit" simultaneously. This means that radioactivity exists on a line between the detectors. As with MRI, combining this information across the many detectors in a PET scanner using clever computer algorithms produces a 3D image, which can be presented in separate two-dimensional slices (Figure 7.2).

The modern PET scan begins with injecting a radioactive tracer into a subject. Depending on which tracer is used, PET can yield an image of the density of a targeted brain substance to which the floating tracer binds (such as the *amyloid plaques* or *tau tangles* associated with Alzheimer's disease), the uptake of glucose (which provides energy to cells) as a means of assessing tissue health (such as detecting tumors, which can have high metabolic demands), neural activity (which also is associated with elevated metabolic demands), or regional cerebral blood flow (which increases with brain activity and thus can be used as an indirect measure to assess brain function). The central idea in functional PET imaging is that parts of the brain that increase in their activity trigger a call for more blood or consume more glucose (each due to elevated metabolic demands), and thus, when using a tracer with radioactive oxygen or glucose, more positron emissions will be detected

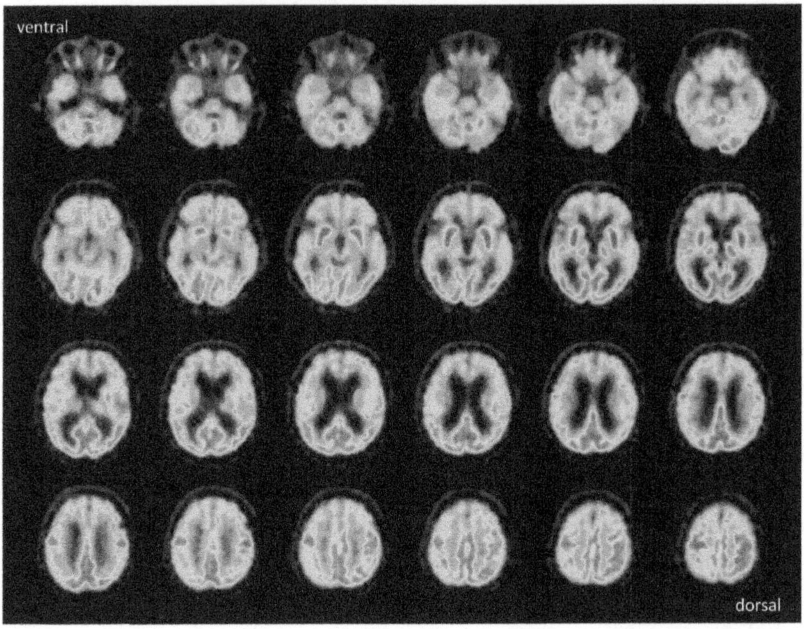

FIGURE 7.2 Metabolic PET scans of human brain in horizontal section from ventral to dorsal.
Source: Adapted from Satoshi Minoshima et al. (2022), "18F-FDG PET Imaging in Neurodegenerative Dementing Disorders: Insights into Subtype Classification, Emerging Disease Categories, and Mixed Dementia with Copathologies," *The Journal of Nuclear Medicine* 63(1): Figure 7. Copyright © 2022 by the Society of Nuclear Medicine and Molecular Imaging.

in those areas simply because more blood is going to them or more glucose is being consumed. In these ways, PET scanning can indirectly measure a change in neural activity. As one of our colleagues once put it, it's a little bit like measuring construction activity in a city not by counting the number of construction sites directly, or even the number of workers or cranes, but rather by counting the quantity and location of food sold from the mobile lunch trucks that visit construction sites.

To obtain information about task-specific brain function (as opposed, say, to whether a patient has a brain tumor), the tracer needs to be administered twice: once while the subject isn't doing anything in particular (the so-called "baseline" or "resting state") or is engaged in a task that does not require the neural process of interest (the so-called "control" condition) and then again when she is performing the task that the experimenters are interested in. Akin to the subtraction technique we saw earlier with event-related potentials, researchers then subtract the first set of readings from the second, presumably leaving the measurements from emissions related only to the function they are trying to tie to the task.

Compared to the electromagnetic field techniques we've already discussed (EEG and MEG), PET can locate with much more precision the areas of the brain calling for more blood when a subject is asked to perform a task, and thus the parts of the brain presumably involved with that task. As with CAT, PET data can be represented on three-dimensional models of the target organ, including the brain. "Slices" of that model can then show the data at a particular level of the target organ. Different levels of "activity"—again, as measured by the change in regional cerebral blood flow or glucose uptake—can be represented on a scale (often depicted as different colors), quickly conveying visually the spatial locations of the detected activity.

Caveat: like the colors used to show storms on weather maps, the coloring on these images is entirely arbitrary—not only the colors used but also the thresholds at which a researcher or clinician decides a signal belongs to one color or the other. Typically, the convention is that cooler colors—blues, greens—are used to show lower levels of measured metabolism or blood flow, and hotter colors—oranges, reds—to show higher levels. But as we have already mentioned, these are NOT direct images of the brain's neural activity; they definitely don't show the brain "lighting up."

The positron-emitting tracers used in PET typically decay in tens of seconds to minutes, so PET scans can give researchers only very coarse information over time as, for example, subjects contemplate, begin, and then finish performing a task in the scanner, or as metabolic processes play out. In addition, different kinds of tracers bind at different rates to different kinds of tissues, and even to different neurotransmitters, which sometimes allows researchers to target the radioactivity to specific structures and chemical pathways. This last feature gives PET a distinct advantage over other detection technologies, especially in clinical and clinically related research. Dozens of different targeted tracers are being used diagnostically to locate anything from bacterial infections to different kinds of cancer, and more are being developed in research. Any pathogen in the body can be detected by PET if a tracer can be found targeted to that pathogen.

PET is also playing a particularly significant role in pharmacology research—it can show the metabolic pathways of any drug being tested as long as tracers can be made to bind to that drug. Many psychotropic medications have been tested and improved by PET scanning, using the technology's unique ability to target particular neurotransmitters. Investigators are also using PET to measure the amyloid plaques and tau tangles of Alzheimer's disease (Figure 7.3).

As with all neural measurement approaches, PET also has limitations. Most importantly, subjects must be injected with the radioactive tracers—at least twice in functional experiments—which constrains how much data can be collected from a subject or patient so as to meet safety standards designed to minimize health risks. This fact inherently makes PET scanning less palatable for some research, where the experiment might require multiple tasks and thus more data. PET is also more expensive than many other kinds of detection technologies. Though like most technologies, the costs of PET scanners have come down since the early days, they are still expensive to buy, install, and maintain. The rapidly decaying tracers are also expensive to buy or generate—they are made with a cyclotron, a kind of particle accelerator—as well as to store and to prepare for use.

PET's spatial resolution is somewhat worse than structural and functional MRI (to which we will turn next). We saw in the last chapter that structural MRI has a spatial resolution of around 1 mm (the thickness of one or two credit cards). PET has spatial resolutions of around 3–4 mm (the thickness of five or six credit cards). And, although the short-acting tracers used to measure regional cerebral blood flow

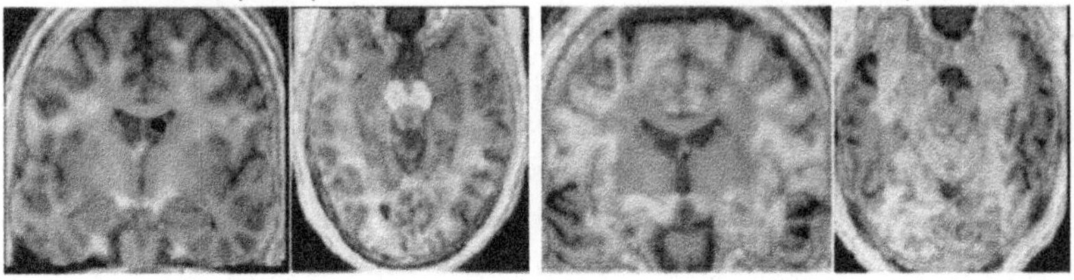

FIGURE 7.3 Comparative tau PET scans of healthy subject (left) and Alzheimer's patient (right).
Source: Adapted from Mormino et al. (2021), "Tau PET Imaging with 18F-PI-2620 in Aging and Neurodegenerative Diseases," *European Journal of Nuclear Medicine and Molecular Imaging* 48: Figures 5a and 6a. Copyright © 2020, Springer-Verlag GmbH Germany, part of Springer Nature.

can give PET some temporal resolution—that is, researchers can see changes over time—it generally takes up to 40 seconds for enough positron emissions to show up on the detectors. Thus, any changes that occur at a finer time scale will be difficult to measure with PET.

For these and other reasons, for most brain researchers PET has largely given way to fMRI as the functional detection technology of choice. But PET remains the king in many clinical settings and for some clinically focused research (e.g., examining whether early amyloid and tau burden in cognitively healthy older adults is related to later memory decline and Alzheimer's disease onset, and examining the brain (and body) for tumors), and it is therefore not at all unusual that PET scans obtained in clinical settings will later find their way into legal settings.

You may also come across a sister technology to PET called *single-photon emission computed tomography* (*SPECT*). SPECT is a form of scanning that uses radioactive tracers that decay very slowly, and thus in effect takes a single snapshot of blood flow (a proxy for brain activity or metabolism) at the moment the tracers happen to emit their photons (gamma rays). SPECT therefore has no temporal resolution, and because it also uses a single detector to detect the emitted photons (rather than coincident detection of two photons), it has significantly lower spatial resolution than PET. But because it is cheaper, and thus more widely available, SPECT may appear more often in legal contexts.

FUNCTIONAL MAGNETIC RESONANCE IMAGING (fMRI)

The MRI systems that we introduced in the last chapter to accomplish structural MRI can be tuned to detect the amount of oxygen in the blood in a particular location in the brain. As with some PET tracers, this technology, called *functional magnetic resonance imaging* (*fMRI*), detects the change in blood flow to a region that follows a change in neural activity, and thus can indirectly measure brain function.

Oxygen is carried in our blood by hemoglobin molecules in red blood cells. Functional MRI takes advantage of the fact that oxygenated and deoxygenated hemoglobin can have different effects on a certain type of magnetic resonance signal. Relative to hemoglobin molecules bound to oxygen, hemoglobin not bound to oxygen has a unique electric charge that can be easily detected by fMRI. Importantly, when activity increases locally in the brain, the supply of flowing blood saturated with oxygen actually exceeds demand, which causes the fMRI signal to increase. This fMRI signal change is called the *BOLD signal*, which stands for *blood-oxygenation level-dependent signal*. It is now used extensively, worldwide, to map and understand human brain function in patients and healthy subjects.

Like PET scanners, fMRI scanners acquire measurements of the signals coming from different volumes of the brain, and PET scans are thus also inherently three-dimensional. Like PET, fMRI can represent these measurements in a three-dimensional model of the brain or can "slice" that model at different two-dimensional levels. As with PET, the color scale used to render the signal intensities of the fMRI data is entirely arbitrary, as is the point at which the strength of the BOLD signal is mapped into different colors on the scale (Figure 7.4.

fMRI has several significant advantages over PET. First, no radioactive tracers need to be injected into subjects, which means that subjects can be tested repeatedly (limited, really, only by their ability to tolerate the confines of the magnet). The acquired spatial resolution of fMRI is around 1–3 mm—better PET's 3–4 mm. fMRI also has significantly better temporal resolution than PET (a few seconds, and sometimes even better, compared to 40 seconds), although of course not nearly as great as EEG and MEG. For this reason, researchers are starting to combine the spatial advantages of fMRI with the temporal advantages of EEG.

As with EEG and PET, "task-based" fMRI studies obtain measurements during baseline (or "control") periods of testing and then during active (or "task") periods of testing, and compare the two in order to determine how the brain's activity changes with task demands. More recent developments use machine learning to detect patterns of activation, from which it is possible to determine some types of

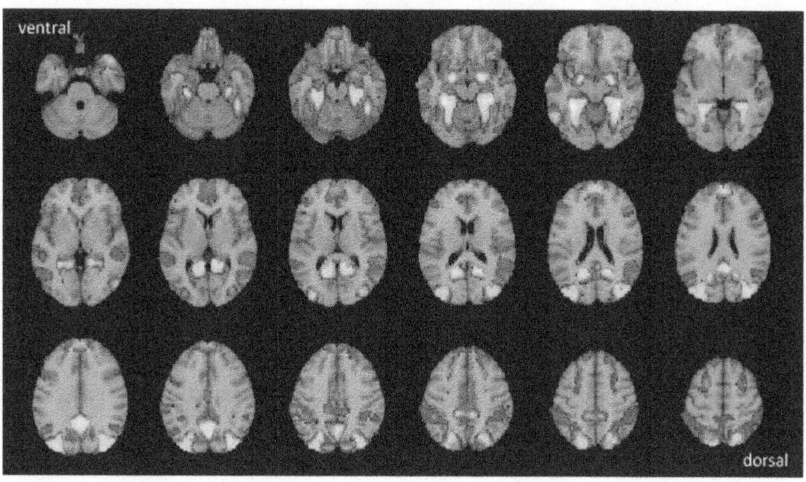

FIGURE 7.4 fMRI scans of human brain in horizontal section from ventral to dorsal. *Source:* Stanford Memory Lab, courtesy Alexandra Trelle, PhD.

mental states (such as what category of object a person is looking at or whether a person perceives a particular face as having been encountered before or as being novel).

While this task-based approach has been very informative, researchers have also noticed that slow fluctuations in fMRI signal occur even during baseline periods. This observation reinforces a key point—the brain is always working even when a person is not engaged in a goal-directed task. Many unexpected and important insights have been gained by examining the patterns of slow fluctuations that occur during these *resting state scans*. Indeed, resting state fMRI is now the dominant tool for measuring how different brain regions fluctuate together over time, providing a way of measuring functional networks in the human brain that relate to cognition and behavior and vary with disease. In a recent resting state experiment, researchers were able to predict which subjects would be harsh punishers in an economic game and which would be lenient punishers, by looking ahead of time only at the subjects' resting state measures of connectivity in certain brain regions.

As we've seen, structural MRI and PET are both very common in clinical settings, and therefore are the brain function detection technologies most likely to be seen in legal settings based on a party's past medical history. By contrast, fMRI is at present less widely used in clinical settings, but it has become the brain-imaging tool of choice for researchers exploring new scientific frontiers (such as its potential for detecting memories or deceitfulness), and it is therefore increasingly appearing in legal proceedings relying on such research.

***

From technologies that measure brain function, we turn in the next chapter to technologies that can actually alter brain function.

8

CHANGING BRAIN FUNCTIONS

"It is not developmentally plausible for a fetus to experience pain prior to at least 24 weeks of gestation. Importantly, even at 24 weeks of gestation, the cortex is still nascent. While nociceptive stimuli can reach the cortex after 24 weeks of gestation, the stimuli are UNLIKELY to generate pain due to the lack of functional connections among critical cortical structures."

Amicus Brief in Dobbs v. Jackson Women's Health Org., filed by Society for Maternal-Fetal Medicine et al. (All caps added.)

"[C]onnections between the fetus's spinal cord and the subcortical nuclei in the thalamus region of the brain begin to form between 12 and 18 weeks. In the past, however, many espoused the unproven theory that conscious fetal suffering was impossible before the development of thalamocortical and intracortical circuitry beginning at about 22 weeks. . . . [But] the mere projection of the thalamus into the cortical subplate area of the brain—which occurs at an early stage of neurological development—COULD BE SUFFICIENT for pain perception."

Amicus Brief in Dobbs v. Jackson Women's Health Org., filed by Dr. Maureen Condic et al. (All caps added.)

INTRODUCTION

Brains are always changing. That's because brains don't just take inputs and turn them into emotions, decisions, actions, and memories. Both the inputs received and their outputs in mind and muscle *change* our brains. You are already familiar with one of the most powerful and ubiquitous ways our brains change: *learning*. Learning French changes your brain. Reading this book will change your brain. Just being alive and having experiences will change your brain. Of course, many of these

Brain Science for Lawyers, Judges, and Policymakers. Owen D. Jones, Jeffrey D. Schall, Francis X. Shen, Morris B. Hoffman and Anthony D. Wagner, Oxford University Press. © Oxford University Press 2024.
DOI: 10.1093/oso/9780197748855.003.0008

changes are microscopic, occurring, for example, as changes in the strengths of connections between neurons that are the byproducts of learning and the substrates of memory. Scientists and clinicians are interested in determining whether and what larger-scale changes are possible, as well as whether it is possible to manipulate brain function in ways that produce better behavioral and cognitive outcomes.

You learned in Chapter 7 how researchers continue to make advances in measuring brain function. In this chapter you will learn about some things that can change brain function—both accidental injuries and intentional interventions. The intentional interventions are used both clinically—to treat brain disorders—and experimentally—to measure their impacts by measuring differences between brains before and after manipulation. In this chapter we will survey four types of brain changes that are likely to appear in legal contexts: (1) brain injury; (2) psychoactive drug effects; (3) surgery; and (4) electromagnetic stimulation.

We will not consider emerging and less common technologies like neuroprosthetics or brain-machine interfaces. Also, we will not cover the neuroscience of learning nor the related topic of brain plasticity—how the brain manages to repair itself as networks of neurons "rewire." The Further Readings and Resources section at the end of this book contains several references to these topics.

BRAIN INJURY

Encased in the skull, surrounded by protective meninges, supplied with blood, and endowed with many ways to repair damaged cells, the human brain can often withstand a lot of jostles without necessarily being injured. Accidentally banging your head against a low-hanging ceiling, for instance, isn't likely to negatively affect brain structure or function, even if it hurts a bit. Nor will the death of a few brain cells necessarily lead to mental decline. But there are many ways in which brain function can be impaired, either temporarily or permanently, and injuries that do so often lead to legal action.

Brains can be damaged by things like blood clots, which can kill neurons by depriving them of oxygen, yielding what is known casually as "strokes" and medically as "cerebrovascular accidents." Tumors, whether cancerous or benign, as well as fluid-filled cysts, can cause brain damage by crowding and compressing healthy tissue. Several degenerative brain diseases, like Alzheimer's, Huntington's, and Parkinson's, lead to loss of function when neurons in various parts of the brain degenerate. And of course brains can also be damaged by trauma, including through concussion from blunt trauma and injuries from penetrating objects, such as bullets.

Regardless of how brain damage is caused, it can sometimes help researchers understand brain function. Seeing (in the days before imaging technologies, almost always by autopsy) what kinds of brain damage, in what parts of the brain, correlated with what kinds of functional problems gave early observers important clues about brain organization and function. Ancient Romans, for instance, discovered—from noticing patterns in war injuries and gladiatorial wounds—that our peripheral nerves come out of the spinal cord at different levels, and enervate different muscles, causing paralysis in different parts of the body. We saw in Chapter 3 that Pierre Paul Broca discovered that the frontal area now named after him has something to do with the ability to speak because he noticed on autopsy that some patients who had difficulty speaking had lesions concentrated in that particular area.

One of the first and most compelling indications of the significant role of the prefrontal cortex in higher order aspects of behavior came from a famous accidental brain injury suffered by a young man named Phineas Gage. Gage was working on a railroad crew in Vermont in 1848, and during a blasting accident an iron tamping rod shot through his head, taking out large parts of his prefrontal cortex. Miraculously, he survived both the accident and the nineteenth-century efforts to stave off infection, with virtually no permanent physical bodily injuries other than the loss of his left eye. But he reportedly underwent profound changes in his personality, including a general loss of inhibition. His friends reported that Gage wasn't Gage anymore. This accident revealed that the prefrontal cortex is crucial to many aspects of our personalities, including responsible decision-making. As a result of this discovered connection between the prefrontal cortex and personality, one now-discredited twentieth-century treatment for some psychiatric disorders was to cut the connections between the prefrontal cortex and the rest of the brain, a procedure known as the prefrontal lobotomy.

Damage to the brain can be localized (like a penetrating gunshot), diffuse (like a traumatic brain injury from a blow to the head), or some intermediate state (like a stroke). Physicians and researchers call a localized area of brain damage a *lesion*, regardless of its cause. You might think that because a lesion is damage to a small area of the brain that its functional impact will necessarily be similarly narrow. But because the brain is so richly interconnected, even a small lesion can have widespread functional impacts. Conversely, even loss of an entire cerebral hemisphere can sometimes have very little or even no impact on function.

Think of any complex device—a car, for example. The tiniest damage to a critical part—such as the battery—can disable the car completely. But widespread damage to noncritical parts—body damage to the hood, for instance, or to parts whose functions can be taken over by other parts—can have little or no impact on the car's utility.

Many researchers are now investigating the neurobiology of concussions, especially those suffered in sports activities, and the immediate injuries and long-term consequences that can come from them. That research is not only leading to efforts at treatment and prevention, it is also part of this long tradition of holding the promise that brain injuries may shed light on brain function.

PSYCHOACTIVE DRUGS

What we put and don't put into our bodies can affect our brains. Nutrition affects both brain development and brain function. So do many drugs.

By the term *psychoactive drugs* we mean substances that we usually voluntarily ingest, either recreationally or at the direction of our medical providers, that can change our mood, perceptions, or thoughts. Our species has long used psychoactive drugs voluntarily to heighten sensation or deaden life's pains, whether physical or emotional.

Psychoactive drugs are often grouped into the following nine main categories (with some examples in the parentheses) based on their chemical natures and their psychological effects:

1. Anesthetics (propofol, barbiturates)
2. Analgesics (aspirin, Advil)
3. Antidepressants (Wellbutrin, Prozac, Zoloft)
4. Antipsychotics (Haldol, Thorazine, Zyprexa)
5. Cannabis
6. Hallucinogens (LSD, mushrooms)
7. Narcotics (heroin, morphine, fentanyl, Percocet)
8. Sedatives/hypnotics (alcohol, Valium, Benadryl, barbiturates)
9. Stimulants (amphetamines, cocaine, caffeine, nicotine)

What is known about how psychoactive drugs work varies greatly by drug, though the ultimate question of how the brain enables the mind to experience these psychological changes remains profoundly unknown. Three examples illustrate this point.

It is well known that cocaine is a dopamine reuptake inhibitor—meaning its effect is to leave more dopamine in the synaptic spaces. It is presumably the excess dopamine that is responsible for cocaine's energizing and pleasurable effects. Opiates (heroin, fentanyl, morphine) mimic a naturally occurring class of neurotransmitters called endorphins, which somehow inhibit pain and produce a general feeling of well-being. The effects of alcohol, by contrast to these other two psychoactive drugs, are metabolically widespread and complex, and not well understood.

There are two clinical classes of pain relievers: anesthetics and analgesics. *Anesthetics* (Greek for "without sensation") can be general, regional, or local, and are typically used to prevent perception of the pain of surgical procedures. They work not just by eliminating or reducing pain but by temporarily eliminating or reducing all sensation. General anesthetics (such as propofol) work at the level of the central nervous system to cause patients to lose consciousness temporarily. Less powerful and/or lower doses of these sedatives are also sometimes used to put surgical patients into a temporary kind of twilight state of semiconsciousness, short of a complete loss of consciousness. The mechanism by which anesthetics cause loss or attenuation of consciousness is not well understood. By contrast, regional and local anesthetics (like epidural nerve blocks or lidocaine) work in the peripheral nervous system to block sensation in discrete areas, usually by blocking nerve transmission from that area. Patients under a local anesthetic remain fully conscious.

Analgesics (Greek for "without pain") reduce pain without reducing or blocking other sensations. Examples include Tylenol (acetaminophen) and aspirin at the mild end and morphine and oxycodone at the stronger end. Some analgesics work by recruiting the body's own naturally occurring endorphins; the pain-reducing mechanism of others remains not fully understood.

One of modern pharmacology's and neuroscience's most important achievements has been the development of drugs targeted to specific brain centers or neurotransmitter systems. We mentioned some examples of these in Chapter 5, including the so-called SSRIs, the selective serotonin reuptake inhibitors, such as Prozac, that work by blocking serotonin reuptake, thereby leaving more serotonin in the synaptic spaces. Somehow, this calms anxiety and eases depression. Another example of neurotransmitter-based pharmacology is the litany of dopamine agonists, antagonists, and reuptake inhibitors developed to treat conditions caused by too little (e.g., Parkinson's disease) or too much (e.g., schizophrenia) dopamine.

An important medical-legal aspect of all psychoactive drugs, whether medically prescribed or recreational, is their addictive properties. We mentioned in previous chapters that researchers think that addiction may be related, in part, to dysfunction of the so-called risk-reward network that seems critical to our assessment of risks and benefits, although the full biomechanisms of addiction remain elusive.

SURGERY

Humans discovered long ago, in Paleolithic times, that some disorders of behavior and discomfort could be treated effectively by creating a hole in the skull. So-called trephination (or trepanation) has been practiced in societies around the world. Historically, though, rooting around in the brain for therapeutic purposes was mostly a hit-or-miss prospect, of which the widespread use of lobotomies in the middle of the twentieth century is perhaps the most tragic and egregious recent example. Because we really don't know what the brain is doing at those intermediate levels of organization where things like cognition and decision-making arise, we don't really know, except by trial and error, how any particular surgery will affect higher order functions. Experimenting with brain surgery on healthy human subjects is of course neither ethical nor permissible today.

But surgeries on animals, and occasionally on human patients who have seriously debilitating brain conditions, have been a rich source of learning about how brains work. In addition to studying the consequences of focal lesions in living animals, by surgically inserting electrodes or other probes into targeted locations in their brains and observing how neural signals vary with behavior, neuroscientists can gain substantial knowledge about how brains function. This has been particularly successful in discovering the neural pathways of basic perception and of voluntary and involuntary (reflex) movement. The locational "maps" represented in the motor and sensory cortical areas, discussed in prior chapters, were largely the product of these kinds of electrode-insertion surgeries, mostly on animals, but sometimes on humans whose brains were directly recorded or stimulated in the course of neurosurgeries aimed at treating a medical condition. Other kinds of therapeutic surgeries on humans have also led to discoveries about brain function. We saw in prior chapters that the hippocampus's role in memory was discovered when the hippocampi in both hemispheres were surgically removed from a patient whose severe epilepsy could not be controlled by medication.

Neurosurgery on humans has made substantial therapeutic progress in the last two decades, in no small part because of the imaging technologies discussed in Chapters 6 and 7, together with sophisticated (often robotic) surgical techniques that are extraordinarily precise. These technologies have made it possible, for example, to remove some brain tumors that were inoperable just a decade ago. Some forms of severe epilepsy, untreatable with drugs, can now sometimes be treated surgically by making several cuts (transections) into the brain tissue surrounding the epileptic source to prevent the seizures from spreading to other parts of the brain.

ELECTROMAGNETIC STIMULATION

In this section we will cover three of the most common electromagnetic human brain manipulation technologies: deep brain stimulation; transcranial magnetic stimulation; and transcranial direct current stimulation.

Deep Brain Stimulation

We mentioned in the preceding section on surgery that much has been learned about brain function by surgically inserting electrodes directly into the brains of animals or of humans with severe conditions. These advances have led to the use of *deep brain stimulation* (*DBS*) for treatment and research. DBS involves a surgical procedure to put an electrical probe into the brain to monitor and manipulate brain function. By directly introducing an electrical current to a particular part of the brain, researchers can investigate various brain functions and clinicians can treat some brain dysfunctions. During the epilepsy surgery described previously, DBS is critical to locating both the areas to be removed and the areas that must remain because they are responsible for critical functions like speech or memory.

DBS can also be used in deeper, interior structures for both research and treatment. The amygdala's role in the fight-or-flight response was established in part by directly stimulating it in animals, which produces a phenomenon called "sham rage" in which the animals bite, claw, hiss, and arch their backs as if they were fighting. In humans, DBS in some deep structures has been amazingly therapeutic. For example, in Parkinson's patients for whom L-DOPA has become ineffective, some have had remarkable and instantaneous relief of the disease symptoms with DBS of a part of the basal ganglia called the subthalamic nucleus. The moment the device is on and sending a current to the implanted electrode, both the tremor and rigidity symptoms of the disease disappear. This relief lasts as long as the current remains on; the motor symptoms instantaneously return the moment the current is turned off. As you can imagine, such dramatic relief can be a godsend to patients with severe and otherwise untreatable Parkinson's disease, whose uncontrolled body movements can be devastating, both physically and emotionally. DBS to treat other disorders such as depression and epilepsy is also being investigated.

The proliferation of DBS treatments and research raises some vexing ethical questions. For instance, who owns the device implanted in the patient's head? What ethical duties are owed to the patient after the research is completed or if the start-up company making the device folds? Questions like these are under active investigation by the National Institutes of Health as it anticipates a need for improved regulation in this area. In addition, implanted neurotech devices will provide novel types of evidence in criminal and civil cases.

Transcranial Magnetic Stimulation

Transcranial magnetic stimulation (*TMS*) is a noninvasive method of exciting or disrupting fairly localized brain areas close to the surface of the cortex. Its operation depends on the reciprocal relationship between electricity and magnetism. That is, just as one can create a magnetic field by moving charged particles through electric circuits, one can also induce or change electrical activity using a magnetic field.

TMS uses pulsed, focused magnetic fields, which pass through the scalp and skull, to influence the signals of the neurons it encounters. With current technology, these magnetic fields cannot penetrate too deeply into the brain, and as a result TMS works better on brain structures relatively close to the surface of the cortex. For reasons that are still being worked out, neural activity in some areas is inhibited by TMS but in other areas is stimulated by it. You can think of single pulses of TMS as creating temporary and localized activation or deactivation of neurons, without having to drill holes to insert electrodes. It has therefore been helpful in establishing or confirming the roles that different parts of the cortex play in different functions, much like the more invasive DBS. So, for example, TMS over parts of the visual cortex can cause a subject to perceive flashes of light. TMS over the motor cortex can cause different muscles to contract, depending on where on the motor cortex "map" the magnetic field is aimed.

By all indications, the effects of single pulses of TMS are temporary, with what appear to be no long-lasting side effects. And these attributes make TMS very useful for human subject research, especially higher order functions of the cortex. Researchers have even found that repeated pulses of TMS over certain parts of the brain can produce long-term and clinically beneficial effects for some disorders, such as depression.

TMS has been an important research tool in examining the roles various cortical areas play in higher functions, like moral judgment and punishment decisions. Two examples will illustrate what a powerful research tool TMS can be in conducting legally relevant neuroscience experiments.

The first example concerns how researchers have linked networks in the brain to various moral decisions, such as whether attempted harm is morally worse than accidental harm. Recall that, generally speaking, the law punishes an attempted (and therefore intentional) harm more than a corresponding accidental harm. So, for instance, we punish attempted murder more than reckless or negligent homicide, even though the latter has left someone dead and the former may have caused no physical harm at all. The law reflects our moral judgment that a protagonist's mental state of *intending* harm is singularly blameworthy. Scientists have used TMS to investigate how the brain has instantiated this distinction between intended but failed harms and completed but accidental ones. Experimental subjects were asked to judge the wrongness of attempted harms compared to accidental harms. Half the subjects had their temporoparietal junctions (TPJs, a cortical area discussed in Chapter 3) inhibited, and the control half did not. Subjects with their TPJs inhibited by TMS judged accidental harms *more severely* than attempted harms, just as young children do before their TPJs are adequately developed. Control subjects whose TPJs were not disrupted judged attempted harms more severely than accidental ones, just like the law does. This dramatic reversal in the laboratory bolsters the conclusion that the TPJ is crucial to decisions that require the assessment of someone else's mental state (that is, the TPJ is part of the Theory of Mind Network).

The second illustration concerns mapping the networks we use to: (1) assess the harm a protagonist has caused; (2) determine the protagonist's state of mind (intentional or something less culpable); (3) integrate those two pieces of information into an assessment of blame; and (4) decide on an appropriate punishment level. A series of papers using fMRI and hypothetical scenarios of wrongdoing found significant correlations between these four distinct decisional components and brain activity in four distinct regions. But because correlation does not necessarily imply causation, researchers subsequently separately used TMS to test the hypothesis that the brain regions identified with these tasks are in fact necessary to the tasks. If, for instance, activity in the right dorsolateral prefrontal cortex (a cortical area that we saw in Chapter 3 is critical to complex decision-making) is causally involved in deciding an appropriate punishment level, it follows that disrupting that region should change how much disrupted subjects choose to punish, compared to a baseline of control subjects who received only sham disruption. And that is precisely what the experiment using TMS demonstrated. As predicted (because the separate decisional components appear to be associated with separate areas of brain tissue), TMS changed how much subjects *punished* protagonists without separately affecting, at all, how much subjects *blamed* those same protagonists.

Transcranial Direct Current Stimulation

Being simple and inexpensive, *transcranial direct current stimulation* (*tDCS*) has garnered renewed interest in recent years. The method involves creating electrical contacts by placing two moist sponges on the scalp over a brain region of interest and some other location on the head (often the cheek). Each sponge is connected to a small device with a battery that generates a weak, constant current that enters one sponge and passes through the brain and head to pass through the other sponge and return to the device. Just what happens in the brain during this stimulation remains an area of active study, but investigators have discovered that tDCS over different parts of the brain can have a variety of interpretable and sometimes useful effects. tDCS is currently being used for both research and clinical purposes. The other brain stimulation methods described in this section are expensive and require professional expertise to deliver. In contrast, tDCS devices can be created at home; indeed, a community of Do-It-Yourself brain stimulation consumers has emerged in recent years.

***

We have to this point provided many of the basics that legal thinkers need to know about brain structure and function, as well as frequently encountered techniques for learning about, and sometimes changing, brain structure and function. We will turn in the next chapter to the crucial topic of separating wheat from chaff. That is: What are the limitations of these various techniques, and what cautions are necessary about how to interpret and understand their results for legal purposes?

9

LIMITATIONS AND CAUTIONS

Sixteen-year-old Joshua Fernandes was hanging out on a Boston street with his friend Crisostomo Lopes, when two gang rivals buzzed them on a scooter, almost colliding with Lopes. Fernandes and Lopes hid until the scooter returned, whose sole driver this time was the fourteen-year-old who had before been the passenger. Lopes jumped out from hiding and pulled the young man off the scooter, and Fernandes shot him multiple times at close range, killing him. At Fernandes' trial for first degree murder, his lawyer attempted to present testimony from an expert on neurodevelopment opining that because Fernandes was only sixteen and his brain was not fully developed, he could not have formed the specific intent to kill. But in an offer of proof, defense counsel conceded that the opinion was "not specific to Fernandes, but in general about the whole concept of adolescent brain development and the underdeveloped frontal cortex," and "whether or not there's even a capacity to deliberately premeditate with respect to first-degree murder." The trial court disallowed this expert testimony, concluding general evidence about brain development could be admitted only if it was accompanied by specific evidence about Fernandes. Fernandes appealed, and his conviction was affirmed.

Commonwealth v. Fernandes, 487 Mass. 770 (2021).

INTRODUCTION

Judges, lawyers, and policymakers trying to use neuroscience to reach legal conclusions must confront three major issues: (1) what particular neuroscientific evidence might mean for the specific legal issues before them; (2) whether that evidence is sufficiently reliable, and in trial contexts, whether it should be admitted into evidence; and (3) how fact-finders should be permitted to use it.

As should now be clear from the first eight chapters of this book, the human brain is an extraordinarily complex organ, and our current technologies are inadequate

Brain Science for Lawyers, Judges, and Policymakers. Owen D. Jones, Jeffrey D. Schall, Francis X. Shen, Morris B. Hoffman and Anthony D. Wagner, Oxford University Press. © Oxford University Press 2024.
DOI: 10.1093/oso/9780197748855.003.0009

to plumb the depths of that complexity fully. Moreover, our current limited understanding of the relationship between brain function and mental states is a major obstacle for the forensic use of neuroscientific evidence. At the same time, and although it is challenging, there are still avenues by which it may be appropriate to use neuroscience in legal proceedings. To navigate that path successfully requires an understanding of the potential pitfalls, and this chapter reviews some of the most important of those pitfalls.

As we saw in Chapter 2, the average human brain contains about 86,000,000,000 neurons. Neurons commonly connect to thousands—and sometimes tens of thousands—of other neurons. As we saw in Chapter 5, these brain "connections" are chemical. And those chemical connections are influenced by the neurons with which they connect, other nearby neurons and modulators like serotonin, all tuned by each person's genetic makeup and environmental history.

When our brains are working on a task, their parts are so richly interconnected that virtually every part is fluctuating in activation at all times. Even during sleep our brains are active in many interconnected ways. Teasing out what each part of the brain is "doing" is both a conceptual and technological challenge. Most neuroscientists believe that what a given brain region is doing will vary depending on what other regions and networks are also doing and how they are interacting with it.

As we introduced in Chapter 2, there is quite a dissonance whenever we contemplate how much we know about the brain. On one hand, thanks largely to the imaging technologies discussed in Chapter 6 and 7, neuroscience has discovered quite a lot about the structures and functions of the human brain, and almost everything we've ever learned has been learned in the last several decades. On the other hand, given the brain's complexity and its inscrutable relationship to mental operations, we still know much less than what remains to be learned. Popular descriptions of neuroscientific discoveries focus on the first message and seldom on the second. "Brain's Deception Center Discovered!" is a headline editors want to run. Who would want to read the story "Scientists Still Have No Idea How Brains Form Intentions"?

As a result, many non-scientists overestimate the ability of neuroscience to answer the fundamental questions all of us would like answered, including why some people behave the way they do, whether we can decode what they know or are thinking, and whether we can predict how they will behave in the future. For many fundamental questions, the human brain remains a dimly lit block, if not still a black box.

But it will not remain so. This is because of expansive global initiatives to understand brain function, health, and disorders. Although knowledge about the brain will remain incomplete, increasingly we will understand where important pieces of the puzzle go. And, as with any complex puzzle, once a few of the right pieces are in place, progress can move more rapidly. The challenge facing the legal use of neuroscience is not whether we know everything, but whether we know *enough*—about a particular brain or group of brains in a particular legal context.

Even with all the advances neuroscience has already enjoyed, and probably even with future advances, there remains difficult gaps between what neuroscience knows and what the law wants to know. And even when neuroscience can reliably answer a legal question, there is one legal context—a trial or evidentiary hearing—in which we must also ask whether probative neuroscientific evidence is probative enough to overcome any unfair prejudice. In the rest of this chapter, we address these legal prongs of reliability, probative value, and unfair prejudice.

RELIABILITY AND PROBATIVE VALUE

We treat these prongs together because in our experience when neuroscientific evidence is misused, it is usually not because the neuroscience itself is unreliable, but rather because it is simply not sufficiently probative of the particular issue for which it is being used. For example, a structural MRI will reliably show shrapnel in a murder defendant's brain, but it is sheer speculation to argue that the shrapnel prevented the defendant from being able to form the specific intent to murder.

This gap between neuroscience and specific legal issues is driven not just by the complexity of brains and the wide variations between individuals but also by the limitations of imaging technologies and other neural data (be they from humans or animals), the relative newness of theories about how brains enable minds, and the murkiness of the legal definitions of mental states.

Good neuroscientists are keenly aware of these complexities and limitations of the methods they use to measure brain function, and they are therefore quite cautious in drawing conclusions from their experiments. These complexities and limitations are commonly part of peer-reviewed evaluations of any submitted publication and are frequently considered by authors when discussing the implications of their results.

The same hurdles apply to drawing legally relevant conclusions from neural data, such as from neuroimaging. But of course in legal contexts there is no comparable peer review. Nothing stands between the fact-finder and the use of neuroscience to argue insupportable conclusions except an informed legislature, agency, bar, bench, and jury pool.

One of the purposes of this book is to educate all of these legal actors on the limitations of neuroscience to unravel the complexities of the brain. Because neuroimaging data, in particular, are increasingly finding their way into statehouses and courthouses, we will focus this discussion on imaging. But we stress that each neuroscience method has its own set of limitations of which legal actors should be aware.

There are many conceptual and technical hurdles in the path from neuroimaging results in a lab to appropriate use in a legislature or courtroom, but here we gather what we believe are ten of the most significant:

1. Anatomical imaging and functional imaging are different.
2. Brain measurement equipment measures only what it was designed to measure.
3. All imaging techniques have limited spatial and temporal resolutions.
4. The appearance of a functional brain image always reflects a number of underlying assumptions.

5. Functional brain images are not pictures of where brain tissue is "lighting up."
6. Brains differ across the population in both structure and function, so generalizing from group-averaged findings to individual cases must be done with caution.
7. Brains are constantly changing.
8. Functional brain imaging is not (quite) "mind reading."
9. Distinguishing "normal" from "abnormal" brains is not simple.
10. A particular brain "abnormality" may or may not be the cause of particular "abnormal" behaviors.

Whenever legal consumers are contemplating the meaning of neuroscientific evidence—whether you are a legislator or regulator considering policy changes, a lawyer trying to get such evidence admitted, an opposing lawyer trying to keep it out, a judge deciding whether to admit it, a juror deciding how much weight to give to it, or even a transactional lawyer trying to decide what it means—these ten points can help guide your deliberation.

1. Anatomical imaging and functional imaging are different.

Anatomical imaging is intended to reveal physical, structural characteristics of the brain. That is, brain features that, as of the moment of the imaging, either are or aren't there. In contrast, functional imaging is intended to reveal differences in how brain tissue is activating under different conditions.

Because the potential combinations of neuronal activations are vastly more variable than the structure of the neurons themselves, functional imaging techniques are generally far more sensitive than anatomical imaging to the specific variables, methods, and protocols used in the scanning and in analyzing scanning results. This strongly suggests that the processes for evaluating the reliability of each kind of evidence should be distinct.

For example, a structural image will almost always be sufficiently reliable, assuming a proper foundation has been laid, to demonstrate that a disability applicant has a tumor in the prefrontal cortex. But to demonstrate convincingly that that tumor is impacting specific types of brain function is another thing entirely, and often beyond the current power of functional imaging. Appropriate clinical testing will be required to better understand the clinical and legal import of abnormalities in brain function.

2. Brain measurement equipment measures only what it was designed to measure.

It may seem an obvious point, but the technologies for measuring brain anatomy or function can only measure what they were designed to measure. X-ray, CAT, and structural MRI are measuring the density and composition of brain material, not their function. So an image from these devices might show a loss of brain tissue or the presence of atypical tissue (e.g., a tumor), but such data provide no direct evidence of loss of (or change to) function. One published clinical article revealed that a patient with no prior functional deficits was missing almost an entire hemisphere of his brain. At the other end of this structure-function gap, tiny changes in brains can have massive functional impacts—strokes, for example, too small even to be seen on PET or MRI.

Conversely, functional MRI and PET do not directly reveal structure, but instead measure indirect proxies of neural activation. Those functional signals are then mapped, as reasonably as can be done, onto what is believed to be the corresponding anatomical structures producing the signals. Put another way, anatomical imaging provides indirect evidence for inferences about brain function, and functional imaging provides indirect evidence for inferences about brain structure.

3. All imaging techniques have limited spatial and temporal resolutions.

As we discussed in Chapters 6 and 7, all neuroimaging techniques have inherent limitations in resolution, both spatial and temporal. Spatial resolution is easy to understand. Compare the image of the moon you see if you are looking through low-powered binoculars to the one you see using a high-powered telescope. The extent to which each device enables observation of fine-grained detail—its spatial resolution—depends on the power of the device being used and is crucial for distinguishing one location in the image from others. Likewise with neuroimaging techniques.

The spatial resolution of the best fMRI and PET technologies is limited. In the case of fMRI, the typical spatial resolution at which data are collected on clinical scanners is 1–3 mm. The spatial resolution of PET is worse—around 3–4 mm. These limitations mean that neither fMRI nor PET can reveal brain processes significantly smaller than the thickness of three credit cards stacked on top of one another (about 2 mm). That may not sound like a problem, but it can be. The activation measured in one 2x2x2-mm voxel in the cerebral cortex is derived from the excitation, inhibition, and modulation of at least 100,000 neurons, each of which may connect with thousands to tens of thousands of other neurons in the brain. So the "signal" measured by these techniques is an average signal that lumps together thousands and thousands of individual signals and is thus blind to any individual neural signal.

Thus, despite their respective powers, these imaging techniques cannot at present resolve the unique contributions of individual neurons embedded in the many circuits, loops, and networks of the brain. And that places some constraints on determining the contributions of the neurons in a given voxel. Nonetheless, because function emerges from population-level neuronal responses, these imaging methods still provide powerful purchase on how function emerges from the human brain.

EEG and MEG have even worse spatial resolutions. As we saw in Chapter 7, the main problem with these electromagnetic detection methods is that, even with the fanciest of detection equipment and source localization analyses, it remains difficult to determine exactly where in the brain these externally detected signals are coming from. The best spatial resolutions of these electromagnetic technologies are around 1 cm (roughly the thickness of twenty stacked credit cards), and the best source localization is achieved by combining EEG and MEG with MRI.

It is in part because of these limits on spatial resolution that human neuroscience is currently hobbled in its understanding of how the brain works at the intermediate level of circuit organization. As you saw in Chapters 3 and 4, quite a lot is known about the function of regions and large networks, because those groupings are big enough to be studied by these techniques. As you saw in Chapter 5, much is known at the microscopic level about how neurons work and communicate with one another across synapses, with most of these insights coming from work in non-human animal brains. But virtually nothing is known about the middle level of brain organization—the smaller circuits that make up larger ones—and that's mainly because of problems in spatial resolution.

Temporal resolution refers to rapid detection of brain changes over time, the way that spatial resolution refers to fine-grained detection of observable physical details. Temporal resolution is a function of the frequency with which measurements can be made and the delay between the brain event at issue (an increase in neural firing) and the direct or indirect measurement (such as a change in blood-oxygen levels) of that neural event.

Here, the electromagnetic detection technologies have a leg up on their imaging cousins. EEG has temporal delays of effectively zero—just the time it takes for the electromagnetic signals from the firing neurons to penetrate the skull and be detected by the devices—meaning we are measuring brain activity almost in real time. It is common to analyze such data in milliseconds (a thousandth of a second).

fMRI and PET, by contrast, each have temporal resolutions that are longer than that, and different from one another. In part, this is because these techniques are indirectly measuring neural activity, either as changes in the BOLD signal that depends on blood flow (fMRI) or as changes in regional cerebral blood flow or brain metabolism (PET).

For fMRI, the key constraint is that there is a delay—called the *hemodynamic delay*—between when a hard-working part of the brain calls for additional oxygenated blood and when that blood actually arrives. The average delay between the brain calling for blood and the peak supply getting there is around 4 to 6 seconds. While it is possible to detect the earliest beginnings of the influx, which provides a temporal resolution of 1 to 2 seconds, those early responses are smaller in magnitude and therefore harder to measure.

For PET, the temporal resolution is even slower—anywhere between tens of seconds and minutes. This is because PET must integrate positron detection over tens of seconds (for measures of regional cerebral blood flow) or minutes (for measures of glucose metabolism) to have an adequate measure of the response.

These amounts of delay may not sound significant, but they can wreak havoc on experiments. In fact, the low temporal resolution of PET largely disqualifies it for experiments designed to measure most mental processes of interest (such as intending an act) and most psychological events of interest (such as a single moment of remembering or lying). For these reasons, along with the others previously noted, human brain function is today most commonly investigated with fMRI.

Even using fMRI, experimenters must always be cognizant of the hemodynamic delay. So, for example, they build in pauses between tasks—such as a blank screen in experiments using computer stimuli, which experimenters call "jitter"—to ensure that the imaging data are not jumbled between tasks. And of course when they attempt to match data to events, they must look back in time to account for the hemodynamic delay, not unlike how we see the flash of faraway lightning before we hear it.

4. The appearance of a functional brain image always reflects a number of underlying assumptions.

As useful as brain images can be, it is essential to recognize that they do not speak for themselves and must be carefully and competently interpreted. Here are three examples.

First, recall that in most functional neuroimaging experiments, as we saw in Chapter 7, researchers attempt the difficult task of trying to tease out the brain areas that might be associated with a given behavior using a technique sometimes called the "subtraction method." To oversimplify, researchers take measurements when the subject is at rest or performing a baseline (or control) task. Then they take measurements when the subject is doing the more challenging target task of interest. And then they subtract the first measurements (at baseline) from the second measurements (during the target task). (In practice, the subtraction method uses more sophisticated statistical tests to determine whether the two measurements significantly differ in signal strength.)

But here's where one underlying assumption comes in. The logic of the subtraction method assumes that the difference in the measurements reveals the neural responses that are associated with the brain processes engaged by the target task, over and above those processes that are shared with the baseline (or that are, in some cases, less required by the task than by baseline). While that assumption is often sound, there are cases in which the demands on the neural processes that are shared with baseline can actually increase in the target task because they *interact* with the other processes in that task. And this can complicate the conclusions drawn or sometimes lead to the wrong conclusions.

For example, in a study designed to identify the brain networks that support attention, a researcher might present visual objects in two tasks—the target task where participants are expected to robustly engage attention and a control task where demands on attention are lower. In both cases, visual stimuli are presented and thus one might assume that neural responses to visual inputs will be comparable across the two tasks—and thus that they may be "subtracted out" leaving only the brain regions that support attention. However, attention often will increase the responses that neurons in perceptual regions of the brain have to sensory input, such as the response of neurons in visual cortex to visually presented objects. As a consequence, there may be increased activation in visual cortex to objects when viewed under high versus low attention conditions. This occurs not because visual cortex is part of a neural network of attention, but because attention modulates the visual cortex's responses to visual inputs (that is, there is an interaction between attention and perception).

A second assumption underlying most functional neuroimaging experiments involves the averaging of results across different individuals. One thing to pay attention to is that the strength of one's conclusions about such averages depends, in part, on the number of subjects in the experiment (and how much data is collected from each subject). While early brain imaging investigations typically acquired brain data from only a few subjects, more recent experiments often involve dozens of subjects or more. Still, these sample sizes are substantially smaller than some psychology experiments or a typical clinical drug trial, which can often involve hundreds or thousands of subjects. But the good news on this problem of averaging is that sample sizes in imaging studies continue to increase, and today, large databases of human brain-imaging data also have been assembled and are openly available to other researchers. Moreover, unlike psychology experiments or clinical trials—which are typically looking at just a handful of outcomes per subject, neuroimaging experiments gather tens of thousands of measurements from each individual brain across all its voxels.

Another thing to pay attention to is that there are both advantages and disadvantages to averaging data across subjects. Before they are averaged, the data from all subjects are typically transformed to a common space (such as the MNI coordinate space introduced in Chapter 2) so that, given different brain sizes, apples can be compared to apples. This allows the analyses to reveal which neural response differences between the target task and baseline are common and reliable across subjects. For this reason, the images published from an experiment commonly represent these group-level differences. At the same time, however, averaging lowers the effective spatial resolution, because the individual variations between brains render it impossible to perfectly align the same brain structures across all participants. And averaging also means that more idiosyncratic neural responses (that is, responses seen in just one or a small subset of studied participants) will often go undernoticed and unreported.

A third assumption about imaging experiments, and other scientific data collection more generally, is that researchers need to conduct statistical analyses that offer an assessment of whether differences in neural responses are likely to be meaningful or could have appeared by chance. You might see this statistical conclusion expressed in something called p-values, which is a decimal expression of the probability that the results appeared by chance. Statisticians sometimes colloquially describe p-values of less that 0.001 (a 1 out of 1,000 chance that the results appeared by chance) as being "very strong evidence"; p-values between 0.001 and 0.01 (a 1 in 100 chance) as being "strong evidence"; p-values between 0.01 and 0.1 (a 1 in 10 chance) as "moderate evidence"; and p-values of more than 0.1 as "no evidence" that the result was different from a chance observation. These statistical characterizations would of course not be dispositive of the legal issue of reliability, but they could certainly be informative.

There are a host of statistical decisions that must be made when handling and interpreting data, such as what statistical techniques to use, how to correct for the number of statistical tests performed, and ultimately what statistical threshold to set for concluding that an observed difference is meaningful. While there are field standards when it comes to these analytic decisions, given the richness of neuroimaging data and variety of analytic approaches, there still can be differences across studies.

In addition, it is important to appreciate that statistical thresholds are scientific conventions; statistical probabilities vary in a continuous manner and so there isn't a meaningful difference between two p-values that lie near, but on opposite sides, of a selected statistical threshold. Neural responses in a brain region that fall just below a statistical threshold might be just as important for the cognition of interest as are neural responses in regions just above the threshold, even though they might not be treated as such. This means that, inevitably, results and conclusions are sensitive to threshold setting. If researchers are overly conservative, fearing reporting of false positives, they might set the threshold too high. That is, the result might be that just one or two regions show up as being differentially active, which could give rise to the mistaken conclusion that the process of interest is dependent on just those one or two regions. Conversely, fearing false negatives, if the threshold is set too low then many regions will show up as being differentially active, and the researcher will have trouble figuring out which regions might be particularly associated with the target task. Moreover, false positives are likely to subsequently fail to replicate in future experiments, adding confusion to the field's understanding of brain function.

Legislators, regulators, lawyers, judges, and jurors being asked to assess the meaning of neuroimaging experiments need to realize that the results of most of those experiments contain these significant assumptions and limitations relating to subtraction, averaging, and thresholding.

5. Functional brain images are not pictures of where brain tissue is "lighting up."

It is common for nonspecialists to assume that the colorized areas of a functional brain image indicate where brain tissue is active, during some task of interest, and that the noncolorized brain tissue is inactive. That is quite mistaken.

As we saw in Chapter 7, the original data from a PET or fMRI scan make a three-dimensional map of the brain, with a signal intensity—that is, a number (not a color)—associated with each voxel. The signal intensities represent indirect measurements of neural activation. (Recall that for fMRI, these numbers depend on the proportion of oxygenated and deoxygenated blood; for PET, the numbers reflect the relative density of particular radioactively labeled substances used in brain processes.) Researchers compare the signal intensity in each voxel when the subject is engaged in a task of interest with the corresponding signal intensity for that same voxel at baseline. These comparisons result in differences that vary across voxels in statistical significance, which can themselves be quantified.

The statistical significance of the comparison between the signal intensities during the control condition and during the task of interest also can be (and sometimes are) represented in a table, according to descriptors of the specific brain regions at which the difference in signals exceeded the statistical threshold. However, it is often more useful to provide a visualization (that is, an image, also known as a brain map—or more clunkily, a *statistical parametric map*)—that depicts the areas of the brains at which different levels of activation exceeded some statistical threshold. Far from representing "no activity," the lack of color on an image represents "no *different* level of activity between conditions."

Of course, a brain image simply overlaid with tons of very tiny numbers wouldn't be easy to understand. So, by convention, researchers replace numbers that vary in value with colors, and represent a scale of those values as a range of colors. When the neural activations during the target task exceed the neural activations in the control condition, and that difference exceeds the statistical threshold, hot colors—such as red, orange, and yellow—are used. When the neural activations during the target task fall below the neural activations during the control condition, and, again, the difference exceeds the statistical threshold, cool colors like blue and green are used.

As you might expect, each experiment bears a legend that shows what value ranges get what colors, and legends vary across experiments. Moreover, the colorized brain maps typically depict regions in which the differences in task and control signal intensities were determined to exceed the statistical threshold; they are not representing the strength of neural activity per se.

Bottom lines: (1) the colors of voxels are not representing the strength of neural activity per se; they instead indicate variations in the probability that the observed differences in neural activation would have occurred by chance, at that location in the brain, between control and on-task conditions; (2) one should never assume that neurons in *noncolored* voxels in the brain were inactive or not differentially active between the task and the control states (because it could be that differences actually observed fell just below the statistical cutoff the researchers selected as the threshold for depicting visually); (3) the colors are themselves arbitrary; and (4) one can't understand what a functional image represents without at least referring to the accompanying legend.

6. Brains differ across the population in both structure and function, so drawing an inference from group-averaged findings to individual cases must be done with caution.

Behavioral and neuroscience research usually aims to produce knowledge about group-level phenomena. For instance, what is the general effect of trauma on the reliability of episodic memory (e.g., eyewitness testimony)? Psychologists might try to answer that question by testing the memories of two groups of subjects—one exposed to trauma during a remembered event and one not. Such data may have direct lessons for policies, such as general presumptions in the law for how to assess the credibility of those who have experienced trauma. But if the fact-finder is required to determine an *individualized* question—whether this particular eyewitness's memory, in this particular case and context, is unreliable because of trauma—then applying the group-based research can be challenging.

Courts confront these *Group-to-individual* (*G2i*) issues in many cases. For instance, in a civil lawsuit alleging that a plaintiff's cancer was caused by a toxin in the defendant's product, it is not enough to show that there is a general relationship, at the group level, between the toxin and the onset of cancer. The plaintiff must show that her individual cancer was caused by the toxin—and not by some other factors. The G2i problem is likewise present with many kinds of neuroscience evidence, where the party proffering it faces the challenge of connecting the group-averaged relationships to individualized legal determinations. Even though there might be group data showing that reductions in activity in a given set of brain regions correlate to an average functional deficit, this does not mean that a given litigant with identical reductions in brain activity suffers from the same dysfunction. Individual clinical measures of function will remain critical.

7. Brains are constantly changing.

It is worth remembering that brains are change machines. Brains change based on: distance from waking, sleeping, or lunch; the internal and external environments they perceive; the new events that happen; and the consequences of the actions produced. Put another way: today's brain is not (exactly) yesterday's brain. Brains change over a day's time, and they also cycle over days. This means that functional images from one point in time may not be reliable indicators of a brain's past or future functioning. This is especially true if there's been a long time between the two events, or an intervening brain-changing event. Functional images, and even structural images, from a teenage brain will look very different from those images once that teenage brain develops into a fully adult brain. Brains might also change quickly in the later years of life. A brain scan two years after a new will was signed may not reliably indicate the decedent's brain health at the time of the signing.

Even events that don't seem terribly significant change brains. You may remember that old commercial showing eggs frying, with the stern narrator announcing: "This is your brain on drugs." Yes, drugs change brains. But so does learning a new language. Or learning anything. For instance, experimenters measuring connectivity by diffusion tensor imaging (DTI, discussed in Chapter 6) in subjects before and after taking a preparatory course for the LSAT—a law school aptitude test frequently used by admissions officers—detected significant differences. Everything we do changes our brains to some degree (often in small ways, but sometimes in large ways; often for short periods, but sometimes for longer ones). The challenge for researchers is to try to correlate certain measured changes to certain changed circumstances. This limitation looms in many legal contexts. The brain of a criminal defendant examined for insanity before a trial will be somewhat different than the brain he had at the time of the offense. The brain of a plaintiff claiming she is suffering from emotional damage from a car crash will be somewhat different from the brain she had at the time of the accident, or the brain she will have in ten years. The question is whether these differences will be great enough to matter to the particular legal inquiry being made.

8. Functional brain imaging is not (quite) "mind reading."

The ability of neuroimaging techniques to reliably detect and "decode" patterns in brain activity is, at times, nothing short of astonishing. Researchers have, for instance, been able to detect when subjects recognize a photograph as depicting an event from their own lives, as opposed to one depicting something new. They can also tell what letter of the alphabet subjects are looking at, whether they are thinking of faces or places, and—sometimes—what object they are thinking about. Some promising techniques are currently decoding the facial features a subject sees in a photograph of someone, and even (very roughly, so far) the characteristics of a video the subject is watching. This is, in a sense, "mind reading." As we mentioned in Chapter 9, experimenters have even had some early successes in distinguishing, by functional imaging alone, whether subjects were acting in a "knowing" state of risk-taking as opposed to a "reckless" state. This work has obvious pertinence to the criminal law's state of mind inquiry, and perhaps even to the civil distinction between negligence and gross negligence.

At the same time, these efforts are not "mind reading" of the sort that many readers might assume when hearing that phrase. There is no technique, at least at present, close to being able to listen in, as it were, to the thinking process. "I think I'll have vanilla, no chocolate, no strawberry—with rainbow sprinkles, on a small sugar cone. And then head over to Grandma's house, taking State Street to Lexington, to avoid rush hour traffic." These ruminations will, in the foreseeable future, remain private, though the integration of brain imaging with rapid advances in artificial intelligence may mean the future is nearer than many of us expect.

It is important that participants in the legal process neither underestimate nor overestimate the power of current technologies to describe how and what people are thinking.

9. Distinguishing "normal" from "abnormal" brains is not easy.

Having an "abnormal" brain could, in some circumstances, be legally relevant. For instance, a defendant might have sustained very severe and widespread destruction of brain tissue as the direct result of a car crash, and might therefore plausibly argue that condition as a mitigating factor at sentencing for a criminal act committed after the accident. Yet determining whether a brain is abnormal in some way, and if so how much, will not be straightforward in cases that lack such severity.

First, variation in brains, across the population, makes it difficult to identify, with precision, what is abnormal. True, there are commonalities between individual brains. Just as most people have one nose, two eyes, and two arms, most individual brains look and perform roughly like one another. Still, and as with all animal organs, brains can vary widely between individuals, in size, shape, structure, organization, and even function. For instance, my dorsolateral prefrontal cortex may be a bit smaller than yours, and may even be a bit closer to the brain's midline than yours. This variability makes categorical line-drawing between normal and abnormal brains very difficult. The central problem is: What *amount* of variance—say 10%, 20%, or more, from some "average" structure size or function—is sufficient to label the brain, or a feature of it, "abnormal"?

But this is only half the problem, and the easy half at that. The bigger problem is that not all abnormal brains result in abnormal behavior, and not all abnormal behavior comes from detectably abnormal brains. Put another way, the *relationship* between observed variance, on one hand, and the cognition and behavior of interest, on the other, can be very challenging to determine. So even an "abnormal" brain may not be abnormal in a way that is necessarily legally relevant.

10. A particular brain "abnormality" may or may not be the cause of particular "abnormal" behaviors.

In the law, causes matter. Judges and jurors are daily called upon to decide whether one party's actions caused damage to another party, or whether some external, internal, or historical condition in a defendant's life caused him to transgress in some way. The relevance and weight of brain scan evidence, introduced in support of a causal inference, is not always clear, for several reasons.

First, you have probably heard the general caution, always important, that "correlation is not causation." That warning captures this straightforward logic: even when one condition regularly seems to appear with another condition, that doesn't mean either is causing the other. For example, between 2002 and 2009, there was a 92.8% correlation between the number of law books published and the number of bicyclists killed in collisions with stationary objects. But no one would seriously contend that either caused the other. One must always look for connective evidence beyond mere correlation before causation may be properly deduced.

Second, inferring causation from brain scans adds some additional (though not necessarily insurmountable) difficulty, because of the complexity of the brain. As systems become more complex, and the number of potentially interrelated causes increases, the problem of mistaking correlation for causation becomes more acute. For instance, in a famous New York case, a man strangled his wife and then threw her body out of their twelfth-floor Manhattan apartment. He wanted to introduce neuroimaging evidence (based on both structural MRI and PET scans) showing he had a very large cyst—called a subarachnoid cyst—in the lining of his brain. In particular, he wanted to argue that the cyst was affecting his prefrontal cortex to the point that it was affecting his decision-making and self-control, and hence his responsibility and culpability for his act. In any new case like this, the court (and jury, if the evidence is admitted) will want to hear about the likelihood that a cyst of this size and nature, in a particular location affecting such a complex organ, could impair normal decision-making and/or impulse control to the extent that such an act might reasonably result.

Third, inferring causation from brain scans can be challenging because of the so-called *base-rate problem*. For instance, because not everyone has been brain-scanned, and because the brain is not visible to ordinary observation, we don't know either the percentage of people walking around with large cysts like our killer in Manhattan, nor the percentage of those people with cysts who throw their spouses out the window. If the former number were very large, and the latter very small, that weakens the case for the causal inference. Without base-rate information, the fact a brain has some additional feature, or is missing a feature or has a seemingly unusual feature, doesn't mean that the condition is causing any dysfunction at all, let alone the particular dysfunction claimed to have caused the particular transgression. As we've already seen, tiny abnormalities can cause massive dysfunction, but large abnormalities can be completely asymptomatic. The effects of any abnormality in the brain depend very much on precise locations with respect to neural circuitry and how much time the brain has to adapt to the change. The devil is very much in the circuit-level details, details that today we know almost nothing about.

The value of neuroscientific evidence, in all legal contexts, will be at its maximum when brain data of any "abnormality" aligns with other evidence that supports an inference of functional loss. A scan revealing a large tumor in the prefrontal cortex might collaterally buttress a clinical conclusion, following a psychiatric evaluation, that someone was legally insane. But the reverse is not true. We would never judge someone as insane on the basis of even a highly abnormal brain scan if clinical and observational evidence indicated that the person in question was functioning quite normally in society on a day-to-day basis.

Armed with knowledge of these ten limitations and cautions, legal consumers of neuroscience will be in a better position to determine whether a particular type of neuroscience is reliably probative of a particular legal issue.

Readers may ask themselves: Won't our structural image showing shrapnel in the brain—the example with which we began this section—be at least *marginally* probative of the question of whether our defendant was able to form the specific intent to murder? After all, doesn't having any kind of demonstrable brain abnormality make it more likely that a brain will not be able to form specific intent? The answer is: not at all. And that's because of the confluence of brain complexity, large differences in individual brains, and our current limited knowledge about some brain functions, like decision-making. With a few very small exceptions (such as damage to the visual cortex or to the brainstem), it is currently impossible to predict whether a given brain, or even most brains, suffering a given shrapnel injury to a given brain area will disable its owner from the ability to form intentions. This may change, as we gather more data and learn more about the circuits involved in the formation of intention. But at the moment, we cannot say that such an injury would even be logically relevant to that issue, though generally speaking the larger the percentage of the brain damaged, the more logical an inference of impairment will be.

But let's say we are convinced that the neuroscience really has something to say about the legal issue we care about. That of course is not the end of the inquiry, at least in litigation contexts, because then we have to ask whether there is any unfair prejudice that might outweigh the neuroevidence's probative value.

UNFAIR PREJUDICE

Even if evidence is probative of an issue, judges must balance that probative value against any unfair prejudice. Neuroscientific evidence may have some unique kinds of prejudices, for several related reasons.

First, as we have already discussed, neuroscience may be especially vulnerable to a mismatching of observed brain abnormalities and alleged behavioral abnormalities. In some sense, this is a general problem in all scientific-legal contexts. We may be prone by the reliability inherent in peer-reviewed science to think it can do more for us than it can. Legal users of brain science seem particularly susceptible to this kind of overconfidence, perhaps because the very complexity of brains and behaviors makes cause and effect suppositions so plausible. "The brain is so damn complex, I could see how a piece of shrapnel could cause a jillion different things, so why not the loss of the ability to form intentions?"

We seem more resistant to these unjustified leaps of faith with other body parts. Before we are willing to conclude, for example, that this particular drug caused kidney failure in this particular individual, we usually need some biological explanation of the relationship between the drug and the injury, or at least epidemiological evidence of cause and effect. But the biomechanisms of the kinds of complex behaviors of interest to the law are largely unknown. Likewise, because of the great individual variations between brains, epidemiological evidence is not as useful when connecting brain losses to functional losses as it has been in other areas of medicine.

There is a second kind of mismatch between neuroscience and law that contributes to the risk of evidentiary overreliance. Precisely because these legal questions seem so deep and complex, and the neuroscience so remarkable, some legal consumers want to see answers where neuroscientists still see questions. Science is all about taking educated guesses—hypotheses—and trying to confirm or negate those hypotheses by conducting experiments. As a result, scientific truth often takes long and winding paths, usually using small steps. Today's truths can well be tomorrow's untruths. But most legal problems must be resolved now, on the best evidence we have, and struggling legal consumers (like jurors) may be tempted to read more into science than is there. This may be especially tempting with neuroscience, which after all can now peer inside the black box that had, until now, been a complete mystery.

There may be a third kind of overconfidence prejudice when it comes to neuroimaging evidence. Though research findings are mixed, some show that ordinary people (like jurors) give neuroimaging evidence more weight than they should. These studies compared trial-like decisions when subjects acquired information only through the testimony of hypothetical experts to their decisions when identical information was conveyed both by testimony and neuroimages, and they found that subjects gave more weight to the latter than the former. This may be a special case of visual processing simply being more salient than verbal processing, but lawyers on both sides of an offer of neuroimaging evidence, and judges ruling on its legal relevance, need to keep this potentially unfair prejudice in mind.

Finally, as with some other kinds of scientific evidence, inferences to be drawn from brain scans are inherently probabilistic. Which is to say: the brain data won't alone prove a causal conclusion, but it may instead be helpful to the extent that such data provide probabilistic evidence suggesting that one causal inference is more likely than another. Most people, including judges, jurors, lawyers, legislators, and regulators, simply aren't good probabilistic reasoners, and unscrupulous legal actors may try to take advantage of these probabilistic blind spots.

***

We turn now to the final chapter, in which we speculate about where this intersection of law and neuroscience might take us in the foreseeable future. We focus on neuroscience advances that we believe might actually have some reliable impacts on legal questions, cognizant that a host of legal actors in the future will continue to do what they have always done: take neuroscience considerably further than the science warrants.

10

WHERE WE MIGHT BE HEADED

On June 12, 2008, a trial judge in India found Aditi Baldev Sharma guilty of murder in the killing of her ex-fiancé, and sentenced her to life in prison. The evidence was strong but not overwhelming: the victim died of arsenic poisoning from a dessert Sharma admitted she brought to him, but the trial judge himself noted that there was no apparent motive for the killing, since Sharma was the one who broke off the engagement, eloped, and married another man. Sharma denied any involvement in the murder, claimed police or the victim's friends planted arsenic-laced leftovers of the dessert in her handbag, and asserted that her ex-fiancé poisoned himself because he was despondent when she told him she had married. The judge found Sharma guilty, relying in part on an entirely passive EEG-based memory detector test the state had administered to Sharma as part of the investigation. The test administrator did not ask Sharma any questions, but instead made narrative statements about the crime, some attributable to Sharma, such as "I bought arsenic." The expert who developed the passive memory detection technology, called BEOS (Brain Electrical Oscillating Signature) profiling, testified that the results indicated Sharma had "experiential knowledge" of the crime, noting that the areas of the brain thought to be associated with memory showed increased activation when these allegedly autobiographical memories were presented to her. A host of neuroscientists worldwide quickly and publicly questioned the reliability of BEOS profiling, and in September 2008 the Indian Institute of Mental Health and Neuroscience declared the technology unreliable.

Maharashtra v. Sharma & Khandelwal,
Sessions Case No. 508/07 (June 12, 2008) (India).

Our book has been dedicated largely to sounding a cautionary note about the uses of neuroscience to answer legal questions. Indeed, the previous chapter surveyed a litany of reasons why current neuroscience is simply not ready to do most of the

Brain Science for Lawyers, Judges, and Policymakers. Owen D. Jones, Jeffrey D. Schall, Francis X. Shen, Morris B. Hoffman and Anthony D. Wagner, Oxford University Press. © Oxford University Press 2024.
DOI: 10.1093/oso/9780197748855.003.0010

work the law is now asking it to do. On the other hand, no picture of the intersection of law and neuroscience would be complete without some educated guesses about where this intersection might be headed in the future, especially given neuroscience's rapid technological advances.

We limit our look at the future to five possibilities: diagnosing chronic pain; diagnosing legally relevant psychiatric conditions; understanding legally relevant mental states; measuring reasonableness; and lie detection. These are of course not the only areas ripe for future advances. But they are five areas where we think the neuroscience might advance in the foreseeable future, and if it does, its legal impacts could be significant. We organize our examples from what we believe to be most likely to happen soonest to least likely.

DIAGNOSING CHRONIC PAIN

A central task of tort law—to justly compensate victims of negligence—has forever been hobbled by science's inability to understand and measure a key component of damage: pain. Pain, both its presence and intensity, has always been a purely subjective matter, and the law has been left with nothing to go on but the word of sufferers and the skepticism of fact-finders.

Chronic pain—typically defined clinically as pain that lasts twelve weeks or more after an initial injury has healed—is even more problematic. It is a common element in tort and disability cases simply because most cases are tried long after acute injuries have healed. But it presents substantial legal and neuroscientific challenges even beyond the challenges of detecting and quantifying pain generally.

Chronic pain is not part of the common experience of many judges or jurors, who therefore naturally have considerable skepticism about claims of pain from injuries that have long healed. This skepticism is only reinforced by what is currently known about the neurology of chronic pain.

Acute pain—what we feel when we hit our thumb with a hammer—is fairly well understood, at least peripherally. The dendritic ends of specialized pain neurons, called *nociceptors,* detect changes in temperature, pressure, force, or chemistry at and near the surface of our skin—the kinds of changes an injury can cause. If the changes are great enough, the nociceptors send an acute pain message to the brain. Because acute pain starts with nociception, methods to detect nociception—like nerve conduction studies—can detect and rule out some forms of acute pain, and can even sometimes pinpoint its sources, which can be important in the treatment of *referred pain,* the pain that comes from injury to or diseases of the spine but is perceived as coming from the extremities.

The peripheral messages of acute pain are ultimately translated into a pain message inside the brain, by processes that are still not well understood. The brain somehow "represents" the pain messages received from the nociceptors, perhaps analogous to how it represents other sensory inputs like sight and sound.

If these nociceptor pain messages are frequent and strong enough, this central brain representation of pain can get stuck, continuing to create what feels like an acute pain message after nociception stops, that is, even after the peripheral nervous system stops sending any pain signals to the central nervous system.

Without appreciating this phenomenon, inexperienced judges and jurors might think chronic pain is psychosomatic or even fabricated. Conversely, of course, unscrupulous plaintiffs or claimants are free to exaggerate or fake chronic pain.

However, neuroscientists may one day be able to reliably detect chronic pain, perhaps even to distinguish it from faking or exaggerating. Using primarily structural MRI on large groups of subjects and sophisticated software to analyze the data, several studies have reported that they are able to detect some kinds of chronic pain by neuroimaging alone, at accuracy levels that are already approaching 80%. Neuroscientists may even be able to distinguish chronic pain currently being suffered from memories of chronic pain that has subsided—a sometimes difficult psychological boundary even for sufferers to appreciate.

There is currently no known cure for chronic pain, and because its treatment often involves the use of opiates, several efforts are underway to attempt to learn more about chronic pain and to develop nonaddictive alternatives to its treatment. Given these efforts, it seems likely that neuroscience will in the future play an important role in resolving forensic disputes over chronic pain. In the bargain, these insights could lead to a deeper understanding of the mechanisms of pain representation in the brain, to better pain treatment and surgical anesthesia, and even to answering questions like whether fetuses or comatose patients or other animals "feel" pain.

DIAGNOSING PSYCHIATRIC CONDITIONS

Not a single condition set forth in the current version of the American Psychiatric Association's Diagnostic and Statistical Manual of Mental Disorders (DSM-5)—the diagnostic bible of forensic psychiatry—is reliably diagnosable by neuroimaging. The sad fact is that, unlike other medical domains, psychiatry is not yet adequately grounded in biology. There are a host of reasons for this, including primarily the fact that the brain's decision-making processes are not well understood, there is so much variation across individual brains, and most mental conditions and diseases seem to be a constellation of symptoms rather than a single condition.

But neuroscientists are making progress toward being able to diagnose some mental conditions by neuroimaging, including conditions such as depression, antisocial personality disorder, and some forms of difficult-to-diagnose brain traumas. For example, recent research has used PET scans to detect the abnormal proteins signaling *chronic traumatic encephalopathy* (CTE) in living former National Football League players. Before this advance, CTE could be diagnosed only after a player's death, at autopsy.

It is not difficult to imagine a future in which brain imaging, blood tests, or other neuroscience techniques will contribute to the diagnosis of some mental disorders. Clinical methods, including observation and neuropsychological testing, will no doubt remain part of the diagnostic process; but neuroscience might become part of, and improve, those clinical methods, just as it has done for the diagnosis of conditions like stroke or brain cancers.

Perhaps more importantly, a deeper neuroscientific understanding of mental conditions promises to advance psychiatry's, and therefore forensic psychiatry's, long quest to become grounded in biomechanism. This could help close the gap between forensic psychiatry and law, not to mention improve psychiatric treatment. The shift to biological biomarkers for mental disorders will also challenge the law's historical distinction between "mental" injuries and "physical" injuries.

UNDERSTANDING LEGALLY RELEVANT MENTAL STATES

The criminal law in most jurisdictions recognizes four culpable mental states: purposeful, knowing, reckless, and negligent. These four mental states cannot currently be distinguished reliably by neuroscience—primarily because of the complexity of forming intentions and the difficulty of inducing them in experimental subjects in legally salient ways. But some neuroscience experimenters have been able to distinguish something akin to the knowing and reckless mental states—the two mental states that give law students and academics, and presumably jurors, the most trouble—by neuroimaging alone. These developments will be unlikely to have wide forensic use; after all, even armed robbers of the future will not likely be donning MRI devices when they commit their crimes. But it could have some inferential uses: for example, if neuroscience could show that at the time of trial a defendant suffered from some condition that prevented him from forming intentions, this evidence could be combined with evidence that the defendant suffered from the same condition at the time of the crime and therefore was unlikely to be able to form the necessary intent at the time of the crime. Similarly, lack of testamentary or contractual capacity could be inferred back to the time the will or contract was executed.

If neuroscience could ever reliably distinguish between mental states, its greatest impact might be in legal doctrine, not practice. For example, it might bolster behavioral research that shows the average person does not make a moral distinction between knowing conduct and reckless conduct and cause legislatures to rethink making distinctions between these two mental states when allocating responsibility and setting punishment ranges. It might guide courts in developing better mental-state jury instructions. It may even present the law with new insights about the defense of intoxication, which in most jurisdictions is available only for purposeful crimes. It is not inconceivable that the law has this exactly backward for some kinds of intoxicants that may affect the brain's risk assessment machinery but not its intent-formation machinery.

MEASURING REASONABLENESS

The law is full of examples where actions are measured against hypothetical objectified standards—the reasonable person in torts, the reasonable expectations of contracting parties, and the reasonable uses of property, to name just a few. The processes of law also require similar idealizations, the beyond a reasonable doubt standard of proof in criminal cases, and in a few kinds of civil cases, being the most prominent example.

Some of these objective formulations may be irreducibly normative. The law punts to fact-finders precisely because, in its accumulated wisdom, it recognizes that it cannot define standards any more finely. But that is not true of all objective legal standards.

For example, much intellectual property law depends on notions of whether a reasonable consumer would be unduly confused by similar products, writings, or trademarks. The "unduly" part of this legal inquiry may be largely normative, but the "confused" part is not—confusion is a mental state. Currently, litigants in infringement cases typically conduct consumer surveys to prove or disprove confusion. These surveys can be expensive and methodologically controversial, and their results are oftentimes ambiguous or otherwise unpersuasive.

Neuroscientists are exploring ways consumer confusion can be objectively measured, not by surveying consumers' subjective reports of confusion but by measuring confusion directly—by measuring the degree to which a survey subject's brain treats two products as being similar. This research is grounded on the well-known phenomenon that when brains encounter stimuli, neural responses generally decline upon repeated presentation. The amount of that decline can be measured, thus providing an objective measure of the extent to which one stimulus—or product—is deemed by the brain to be a mere repeat of a prior stimulus—or product.

Even in areas where the "reasonableness" inquiry seems irreducibly normative, neuroscience may shed light on how the law describes the inquiry, and in particular how, and whether, jury instruction definitions of reasonableness might be written to produce more reliable outcomes.

LIE DETECTION

Traditional polygraphy, which uses various physiological measurements to try to distinguish truth-telling from lying—pulse and respiration rates, blood pressure, skin perspiration, pupil dilation—has been around in some form since the early 1900s, and it remains generally inadmissible in federal courts and almost every state court. The current state of the research supports this skepticism. A 2003 National Academy of Sciences report found that significant problems in inter-rater reliability—differences between different polygraphers—made it impossible to make any general assessment of the reliability of the technology.

A new generation of polygraphy is now attempting to enter the field—using various neuroimaging techniques, including EEG and fMRI. Alas, according to a 2014 meta-study sponsored by the MacArthur Foundation, lie detection by neuroimaging remains fraught with so many problems, including ambiguous experimental design and a lack of inter-rater reliability, that the method cannot be said to have any known reliability rate, let alone a rate high enough to satisfy the requirements of the courtroom. It is conceivable that some of these problems might be overcome in the future, though even if they are, there are two problems that seem insurmountable: countermeasures and the problem of the invited lie.

Because neuroimaging results can be so sensitive to a whole host of conditions, neuroimaging by lie detection promises to ignite a war of countermeasures and counter-countermeasures. Similar wars happened with traditional polygraphy, but it is probably much easier to infect neuroimaging results. Just wiggling a finger may do it.

And even if the technology can stay one step ahead of the countermeasures, there seems to be an intractable problem that goes to the very heart of the whole question of whether any lie detection method can be reliably studied. Lie detection experiments typically invite or sometimes even direct subjects to lie. Until researchers can give us comfort that these permitted lies are psychologically close enough to real-world lies, these experiments may never tell us anything about the ability of any technology to detect real-world lies.

If all of these problems are somehow overcome at some time in the future, and reasonably reliable but far from perfect lie detection methods developed, at some point the law may have to ask itself: Would we prefer a 70% reliable lie detector to 50% or even 60% reliable judges or juries (several experiments have shown that people are at about chance in their ability to detect lies from truth-telling)?

Even if courts remain skeptical of lie detection by neuroimaging, as we believe they should be based on current science, there is a host of pre-court and other non-court legal uses, including police investigations, employment interviews, and security clearances, where neuroimaging will begin to displace the traditional polygraphy that is already being done in all these areas.

AFTERWORD

Because we can look inside human brains without killing their owners, we have learned enormous amounts about how brains are built and how they work. We know a great deal about how individual neurons work and communicate with each other and with other body parts, and we also know a great deal about large functional brain regions, like the visual cortex. But we don't know much about how neurons organize into the circuits that form the larger regions and brain networks, primarily because of the current spatial limitations of neuroscience technology. Progress at this intermediate level of brain organization, when combined with that at the other levels, promises to answer many of the most tantalizing neuroscience questions, including: how we translate sensory information into memories; how we convert senses and memories into action plans; how we integrate emotion, motivation, cognition, moral judgment, and inhibition into intentions and then actions; and how different brain injuries, diseases, and conditions, like being under the influence of certain substances, affect that integration.

People from every walk of life, not just legal actors, are understandably eager to use scientific knowledge for their own good, and policymakers are eager to use it for the common good. In their eagerness to apply neuroscience to law, many legal consumers may be lured into seeing the cup of brain knowledge as half full instead of half empty. For others with a more cynical bent, it may be tempting to see the cup as mostly empty. We know a lot about the brain, and some of what we know is properly informing the law—for example, some legally relevant clinical diagnoses now include neuroimages as part of the diagnostic toolbox—even though most legal questions, alas, remain beyond the current grasp of neuroscience.

As with most innovations—like electricity, cars, and the internet—neuroscience must be used carefully to avoid doing more harm than good. By the same token, the inquiry should never be "Is neuroscience perfect?" but rather "Is neuroscience reliably better than current alternatives?" Fortunately, the law has a long tradition of balancing the probative value of imperfect information against its risk of unfair prejudice. In this sense, neuroscience may be at its least dangerous when it is being tested in legal domains, compared to less rigorous domains, like the media.

Readers now familiar with the basics of what is currently known about the human brain should be in a good position to separate legally helpful neuroscience from legally unhelpful or even misleading neuroscience. Perhaps more importantly, as we learn more and more about the brain, readers familiar with the present state of brain knowledge, and its limitations, should be better able to judge whether new neuroscience will shed any new legal light.

FURTHER READINGS AND RESOURCES

Those interested in learning more about the topics covered in this book may find the following readings and resources useful. The following materials are organized by subject area.

LEGAL RESOURCES

To stay up to date:

- To keep you up to date on recent happenings in neurolaw, the complimentary *Neurolaw News* listserv periodically circulates new developments in publications, conferences, cases, and the like. Sign up to receive it at http://www.lawneuro.org/listserv.php. Past editions available at http://www.lawneuro.org/news.php
- A comprehensive, searchable, sortable bibliography of publications in Law and Neuroscience is available online at http://www.lawneuro.org/bibliography.php
- Follow the research of the MacArthur Foundation Research Network on Law and Neuroscience here: https://www.lawneuro.org
- The Center for Law, Brain & Behavior at Massachusetts General Hospital also provides law and neuroscience resources at https://clbb.mgh.harvard.edu

On law and neuroscience, generally:

- Jones, O.D., Schall, J.D., and Shen, F.X., *Law and Neuroscience* (2nd ed., Wolters Kluwer, 2021).
- The MacArthur Foundation Research Network on Law and Neuroscience, *Law & Neuroscience: What, Why, and Where to Begin* (MacArthur Foundation, 2016).
- Jones, O.D., Buckholtz, J., Schall, J.D., and Marois, R., "Brain Imaging for Legal Thinkers: A Guide for the Perplexed," *Stanford Technology Law Review*, 5 (2009), 1.
- Jones, O.D. and Wagner, A.D., "Law and Neuroscience: Progress, Promise, and Pitfalls," in D. Pöppel, G. Mangun, and M. Gazzaniga, eds., *The Cognitive Neurosciences* (6th ed., 2019), 1015–1025.
- Greely, H.T., and Wagner, A.D., "Reference Guide on Neuroscience," in Federal Judicial Center, *Reference Manual on Scientific Evidence* (3rd ed., National Academies Press, 2011), 747–812.
- Shen, F.X., "The Overlooked History of Neurolaw," *Fordham Law Review*, 85 (2011), 667.
- Chandler, J.A., Harrel, N., and Potkonjak, T., "Neurolaw Today: A Systematic Review of the Recent Law and Neuroscience Literature," *International Journal of Law and Psychiatry*, 65 (2018), 1.
- Hoffman, M.B., "Nine Neurolaw Predictions," *New Criminal Law Review*, 21 (2018), 212.

- Jones, O.D., "Seven Ways Neuroscience Aids Law," in A. Battro, S. Dehaene, and W. Singer, eds., *Neurosciences and the Human Person: New Perspectives on Human Activities* (Scripta Varia, 2013), 1–14.
- Jones, O.D., "The Future of Law and Neuroscience," *William & Mary Law Review*, 63 (2022), 1317.
- Shen, F.X., "Law and Neuroscience 2.0," *Arizona State Law Journal*, 48 (2016), 1043.
- Ligthart, S., van Toor, D., Kooijmans, T., Douglas, T., Meynen, G., eds., *Neurolaw: Advances in Neuroscience, Justice & Security* (Palgrave Macmillan, 2021).
- Alces, P., *The Moral Conflict of Law and Neuroscience* (University of Chicago Press, 2018).

International perspectives:

- D'Aloia, A., and Errigo, M.C., eds., *Neuroscience and Law: Complicated Crossings and New Perspectives* (Springer Cham, 2020).
- Spranger, T.M., *International Neurolaw: A Comparative Analysis* (Springer, 2012).
- Desmoulin-Canselier, S., "France in the Neurolaw Era: Brain Imaging in French Civil Litigation," *Droit et Société*, 101 (2019), 117.

Medical references written for legal audiences:

- Dox, Ida C., Eisner, Gilbert M., Melloni, B.J., and Melloni, J.L., *Attorney's Illustrated Medical Dictionary* (Thompson West, 2015).
- Moore, P., Brifanci, S., and Worthington, A., *Neuropsychological Aspects of Brain Injury Litigation: A Medicolegal Handbook for Lawyers and Clinicians* (Routledge, 2022).
- Bernard, P.G., *Closed Head Injury: A Clinical Source Book* (5th ed., Juris Publishing, 2016).
- Hubbard, J.E., and Hodge, S.D., *Head Trauma and Brain Injury for Lawyers* (American Bar Association, 2016).

Neuroscience in courts and legislatures:

- Farahany, N.A., "Neuroscience and Behavioral Genetics in U.S. Criminal Law: An Empirical Analysis," *Journal of Law and the Biosciences*, 2 (2015), 485.
- Shen, F.X., "Neurolegislation: How U.S. Legislators Are Using Brain Science," *Harvard Journal of Law and Technology*, 29 (2015), 495.
- Moriarty, J., "Neuroimaging Evidence in U.S. Courts," in B. Brozek, F. Shen, N. Vincent, and J. Hage, eds., *Neuroimaging Evidence in the United States, in Law and Mind: At the Intersection of Law and the Cognitive Sciences* (Cambridge University Press, 2021), 370–411.
- Chandler, J.A., "The Use of Neuroscientific Evidence in Canadian Criminal Proceedings," *Journal of Law and Bioscience*, 2 (2015), 550.

Neuroscience and criminal law:

- Morse, S.J., and Roskies, A.L., *A Primer on Criminal Law and Neuroscience: A Contribution of the Law and Neuroscience Project, Supported by the MacArthur Foundation* (Oxford University Press, 2013).
- Moore, M.S., *Mechanical Choices: The Responsibility of the Human Machine* (Oxford University Press, 2020).
- Ryberg, J., *Neurointerventions, Crime, and Punishment: Ethical Considerations* (Oxford University Press, 2019).

- Denno, D.W., "Neuroscience and the Personalization of Criminal Law," *University of Chicago Law Review*, 86 (2019), 359.

GENERAL NEUROSCIENCE RESOURCES

Basic introductions to the brain:

- Carter, R., *The Human Brain Book: An Illustrated Guide to its Structure, Function, and Disorders* (DK, 2019).
- Ward, J., *The Student's Guide to Cognitive Neuroscience* (4th ed., Routledge, 2019).
- Jones, O.D., Schall, J.D., and Shen, F.X., "Part II: Fundamentals of Cognitive Neuroscience," in *Law and Neuroscience* (2nd ed., Aspen Publishing, 2021), 69–150.

Introductory college-level textbooks:

- Kalat, J.W., *Biological Psychology* (14th ed., Cengage, 2023).
- Banich, M.T., and Compton, R.J., *Cognitive Neuroscience* (4th ed., Cambridge University Press, 2018).

More advanced college- and graduate-level textbooks:

- Purves, D., LaBar, K.S., Platt, M.L., Woldorff, M., Cabeza, R., and Huettel, S., *Principles of Cognitive Neuroscience* (2nd ed., Oxford University Press, 2012).
- Bear, M.F., Connors, B.W., and Paradiso, M.A., *Neuroscience: Exploring the Brain* (4th ed., Jones & Bartlett, 2020).
- Gazzaniga, M., Ivry, R.B., and Mangun, G.R., *Cognitive Neuroscience: The Biology of the Mind* (5th ed., W.W. Norton & Company, 2018).
- Purves, D., Augustine, G.J., Fitzpatrick, D., Hall, W.C., LaMantia, A.-S., Mooney, R.D., Platt, M.L., and White, L., *Neuroscience* (6th ed., Oxford University Press, 2017).
- Kandel, E., Schwartz, J., and Jessell, T., *Principles of Neural Science* (6th ed., McGraw Hill, 2021).
- Squire, L., Spitzer, N., Berg, D., Bloom, F., du Lac, S., and Ghosh, A., *Fundamental Neuroscience* (4th ed., Academic Press, 2012).

Limbic system, emotions, and memory:

- Squire, L., and Kandel, E., *Memory: From Mind to Molecules* (Holt Paperbacks, 2008).
- Schacter, D.L., *The Seven Sins of Memory Updated Edition: How the Mind Forgets and Remembers* (Mariner Books, 2021).
- Corkin, S., *Permanent Present Tense: The Unforgettable Life of the Amnesic Patient* (Penguin Books, 2013).
- Schacter, D.L., and Loftus, E., "Memory and Law: What Can Cognitive Neuroscience Contribute?," *Nature Neuroscience*, 16 (2013), 119.
- Lacy, J.W., and Stark, E.L., "The Neuroscience of Memory: Implications for the Courtroom," *Nature Reviews Neuroscience*, 14 (2013), 649.
- Whalen, P.J., and Phelps, E.A., *The Human Amygdala* (The Guilford Press, 2009).
- Phelps, E.A., "Emotion and Cognition: Insights from Studies of the Human Amygdala," *Annual Review of Psychology*, 57 (2006), 27.
- Adolphs, R., and Anderson, D.J., *The Neuroscience of Emotion: A New Synthesis* (Princeton University Press, 2018).
- Barrett, L.F., *How Emotions Are Made: The Secret Life of the Brain* (Mariner, 2018).

Basal ganglia and addiction:

- Timmons, C.R., and Hamilton, L.W., *Drugs, Brains, and Behavior: The Science of Addiction* (National Institute on Drug Abuse, 2018).
- Rangel, A., Camerer, C., and Montague, P.R., "A Framework for Studying the Neurobiology of Value-Based Decision Making," *Nature Reviews Neuroscience*, 9 (2008), 545.

Online resources for introductions to the brain:

- The Society for Neuroscience curates ***Brain Facts*** at https://www.brainfacts.org. This includes an interactive and educational 3D brain at https://www.brainfacts.org/3d-brain
- Another 3D brain rendering with educational information is ***BrainTutor***, produced by a company called Brain Innovation, which develops scientific and educational software in the field of brain imaging at https://www.brainvoyager.com/webapps/braintutor/BrainTutor.html
- ***Neurosynth*** is a web-based platform that synthesizes thousands of published articles reporting functional magnetic resonance imaging (fMRI) data. You can use over 1,300 terms to search through nearly 510,000 distinct activations reported in over 14,000 studies to show functional connectivity and coactivation maps for over 150,000 brain locations. Also, you can view whole-brain maps of expression levels of numerous human genes. With your cursor, you can also navigate locations in the brain and learn the name of a given structure, the conditions in which that region is activated, and the other brain regions with which it is associated. https://neurosynth.org

Brain plasticity:

- Doidge, N., *The Brain That Changes Itself: Stories of Personal Triumph from the Frontiers of Brain Science* (Penguin Life, 2007).
- Costandi, M., *Neuroplasticity* (MIT Press, 2016).
- Chalupa, L.M., Berardi, N., Caleo, M., Resta, L.G., and Pizzorusso, T., *Cerebral Plasticity* (MIT Press, 2011).

NEUROIMAGING

Neuroimaging generally:

- Jenkinsen, M., and Chappell, M., *An Introduction to Neuroimaging Analysis* (Oxford University Press, 2018).
- Jones, O.D., Buckholtz, J., Schall, J.D., and Marois, R., "Brain Imaging for Legal Thinkers: A Guide for the Perplexed," *Stanford Technology Law Review*, 5 (2009), 1.
- Sporns, O., *Discovering the Human Connectome* (MIT Press, 2016).

X-ray and CAT:

- Nitske, W.R., *The Life of Wilhelm Conrad Roentgen, Discoverer of the X-Ray* (University of Arizona Press, 1971).
- Kalender, W.A., "X-ray Computed Tomography," *Physics in Medicine & Biology*, 51 (2006), R29.

EEG:

- Luck, S.J., *An Introduction to Event-Related Potential Technique* (2nd ed., MIT Press, 2014).

- Luck, S.J., and Kappenman, E.S., *The Oxford Handbook of Event-Related Potential Components* (Oxford University Press, 2011).
- Budzynski, T.H., Budzynski, H.K., Evans, J.R., and Abarbanel, A., *Introduction to Quantitative EEG and Neurofeedback: Advanced Theory and Applications* (Academic Press, 2009).

PET and SPECT:

- Herholz, K., Herscovitch, P., and Heiss, W-D., *NeuroPET: Position Emission Tomography in Neuroscience and Clinical Neurology* (Springer, 2004).
- Valk, P.E., Delbeke, D., Bailey, D.L., Townsend, D.W., and Maisey, M.N., *Positron Emission Tomography: Clinical Practice* (2006 ed., Springer, 2006).
- Van Heertum, R.L., Tikofsky, R.S., and Ichise, M., *Functional Cerebral SPECT and PET Imaging* (4th ed., Lippincott Williams & Wilkins, 2012).
- Posner, M.J., and Raichle, M.E., *Images of Mind* (WH Freeman, 1997).

MRI:

- Dale, B., Brown, M., and Semelka, R., *MRI: Basic Principles and Applications* (5th ed., John Wiley & Sons, 2015).
- Plewes, D.B., and Kucharczyk, W., "Physics of MRI: A Primer," *Journal of Magnetic Resonance Imaging,* 35 (2012), 1038.
- Rakić, M., Cabezas, M., Kushibar, K., Oliver, A., and Lladó, X., "Improving the Detection of Autism Spectrum Disorder by Combining Structural and Functional MRI Information," *NeuroImage: Clinical,* 25 (2020), 1.

DTI:

- O'Donnell, L., and Westin, C.-F., "An Introduction to Diffusion Tensor Image Analysis," *Neurosurgery Clinics,* 22 (2011), 185.
- Mayo, C.D., Garcia-Barrera, M.A., Mazerolle, E.L., Ritchie, L.J., Fisk, J.D., and Gawryluk, J.R., "Relationship Between DTI Metrics and Cognitive Function in Alzheimer's Disease," *Frontiers in Aging Neuroscience,* 10 (2019), 436.

fMRI:

- Huettel, S.A., Song, A.W., and McCarthy, G., *Functional Magnetic Resonance Imaging* (3rd ed., Oxford University Press, 2014).
- Aguirre, G., "The Fundamentals of fMRI," *Center for Functional Neuroimaging* (2004).
- Papanicolaou, A.C., *The Oxford Handbook of Functional Brain Imaging in Neuropsychology and Cognitive Neurosciences* (Oxford University Press, 2017).
- Filippi, M., and Agosta, F., *Imaging Dementia: Essentials for Clinical Practice* (Springer, 2021).

BRAIN INJURY

- Jones, O.D., Schall, J.D., and Shen, F.X., "Brain Injury," in *Law and Neuroscience* (2nd ed., Aspen Publishing, 2021), 347–396.
- Rao, V., and Vaishnavi, S., *The Traumatized Brain: A Family Guide to Understanding Mood, Memory, and Behavior after Brain Injury* (Johns Hopkins Press, 2015).

- Zollman, F., *Manual of Traumatic Brain Injury: Assessment and Management* (Springer, 2021).
- Sacks, O., *The Man Who Mistook His Wife for a Hat: And Other Clinical Tales* (Summit Books, 1998).
- Davis, K., *The Brain Defense: Murder in Manhattan and the Dawn of Neuroscience in America's Courtrooms* (Penguin Press, 2017).

BRAIN MODULATION

Drugs:

- Prus, A., *Drugs and the Neuroscience of Behavior: An Introduction to Psychopharmacology* (3rd ed., SAGE Publications, 2020).
- Quenzer, L.F., and Meyer, J.S., *Psychopharmacology Drugs, the Brain & Behavior* (2nd ed., Oxford University Press, 2018).
- Iversen, L., Iversen, S., Bloom, F., and Roth, R., *Introduction to Neuropsychopharmacology* (Oxford University Press, 2008).

Neurosurgery and deep brain stimulation:

- Chandler, J.A., Cabrera, L.Y., Fecteau, S., Fins, J.J., Guinjoan, S., Hamani, C., Herrera-Ferrá, K., Honey, C.M., Illes, J., Kopell, B.H., Lipsman, N., McDonald, P.J., Mayberg, H.S., Nadler, R., Nuttin, B., Oliveira-Maia, A.J., Rangel, C., Ribeiro, R., Salles, A., and Wu, H., "International Legal Approaches to Neurosurgery for Psychiatric Disorders," *Frontiers in Human Neuroscience*, 14 (2021), 1.
- Nadler, R., and Chandler, J.A., "Legal Regulation of Psychosurgery: A Fifty-State Survey," *Journal of Legal Medicine*, 39 (2019), 335.
- Sheth, S.A., and Mayberg, H.S., "Deep Brain Stimulation for Obsessive-Compulsive Disorder and Depression," *Annual Review of Neuroscience*, 46 (2023), 341.
- Suthana, N., and Fried, I., "Deep Brain Stimulation for Enhancement of Learning and Memory," *Neuroimage*, 85 (2014), 996.

Transcranial direct stimulation:

- Knotkova, H., Nitsche, M.A., Bikson, M., and Woods, A.J., *Practical Guide to Transcranial Direct Current Stimulation: Principles, Procedures and Applications* (Springer, 2019).

LIMITATIONS AND CAUTIONS

General cautions:

- Cacioppo, J.T., Berntson, G.G., Lorig, T.S., Norris, C.J., Rickett, E., and Nusbaum, H., "Just Because You Are Imaging the Brain Doesn't Mean You Can Stop Using Your Head: A Primer and Set of First Principles," *Journal of Personality and Social Psychology*, 85 (2003), 650.
- Morse, S.J., "Brain Overclaim Syndrome and Criminal Responsibility: A Diagnostic Note," *Ohio State Journal of Criminal Law*, 3 (2005), 397.
- Morse, S.J., "Neurohype and the Law: A Cautionary Tale," in A. Raz and R.T. Thibault, eds., *Casting Light on the Dark Side of Brain Imaging* (Elsevier Science & Technology, Academic Press, 2019), 31–35.
- Poldrack, R.A., *The New Mind Readers: What Neuroimaging Can and Cannot Reveal about Our Thoughts* (Princeton University Press, 2018).

- Jones, O.D., Buckholtz, J.W., Schall, J.D., and Marois, R., "Brain Imaging for Legal Thinkers: A Guide for the Perplexed," *Stanford Technology Law Review* 5 (2009), 1.
- Poldrack, R.A., and Farah, M.J., "Progress and Challenges in Probing the Human Brain," *Nature*, 526 (2015), 371.
- Poldrack, R.A., *The New Mind Readers: What Neuroimaging Can and Cannot Reveal about Our Thoughts* (Princeton University Press, 2020).
- Shen, F.X., Wolf, S.M., Gonzalez, R.G., and Garwood, M., "Ethical Issues Posed by Field Research Using Highly Portable and Cloud-Enabled Neuroimaging," *Neurion*, 105 (2020), 771.

Individual brain variation:

- Dubois, J., and Adolphs, R., "Building a Science of Individual Differences from fMRI," *Trends in Cognitive Sciences*, 20 (2016), 425.
- Michon, K.J., Khammash, D., Simmonite, M., Hamlin, A.M., and Polk, T.A., "Person-specific and Precision Neuroimaging: Current Methods and Future Directions," *Neuroimage*, 263 (2022), 1.

Causation and reverse inference:

- Calzavarini, F., and Cevolani, G., "Abductive Reasoning in Cognitive Neuroscience: Weak and Strong Reverse Inference," *Synthese*, 200 (2022), 70.
- Faigman, D.L., Monahan, J., and Slobogin, C., "Group to Individual (G2i) Inference in Scientific Expert Testimony," *University of Chicago Law Review*, 81 (2014), 417.
- Kriegeskorte, N., Simmons, W.K., Bellgowan, P., and Baker, C.I., "Circular Analysis in Systems Neuroscience: The Dangers of Double Dipping," *Nature Neuroscience*, 12 (2009), 535.
- Poldrack, R., "Can Cognitive Processes Be Inferred from Neuroimaging Data?," *Trends in Cognitive Sciences*, 10 (2006), 59.

BRAIN-MACHINE (BRAIN-COMPUTER) INTERFACES

General overview:

- Kurzweil, R., *The Singularity Is Near: When Humans Transcend Biology* (Penguin Books, 2006).
- Nicolelis, M., *Beyond Boundaries: The New Neuroscience of Connecting Brains with Machines—And How It Will Change Our Lives* (Macmillan, 2011).
- Horstman, J., *The Scientific American Brave New Brain: How Neuroscience, Brain-Machine Interfaces, Neuroimaging, Psychopharmacology, Epigenetics, the Internet, and Our Own Minds Are Stimulating and Enhancing the Future of Mental Power* (Jossey-Bass, 2010).
- Gay, M., *The Brain Electric: The Dramatic High-Tech Race to Merge Minds and Machines* (Macmillan, 2015).
- Urban, T., *Neuralink and the Brain's Magical Future* (Wait But Why, 2017).
- Nam, C.S., Nijholt, A., and Lotte, F., eds., *Brain-Computer Interfaces Handbook: Technological and Theoretical Advances* (CRC Press, 2018).

Ethical and legal considerations:

- Wu, S.S., and Goodman, M., "Neural Devices Will Change Humankind: What Legal Issues Will Follow?," *SciTech Lawyer*, 8 (2012), 12.

- Klein, E., and Rubel, A., "Privacy and Ethics in Brain-Computer Interface Research," in C. Nam, A. Nijholt, and F. Lotte, eds., *Brain-Computer Interfaces Handbook: Technological and Theoretical Advances* (CRC Press, 2018), 653.
- Bess, M., *Our Grandchildren Redesigned: Life in Bioengineered Society of the Near Future* (Beacon Press, 2015).
- Harari, Y.N., *Homo Deus: A Brief History of Tomorrow* (HarperCollins, 2017).
- Kreitmair, K.V., "Dimensions of Ethical Direct-To-Consumer Neurotechnologies," *AJOB Neuroscience*, 10 (2019), 152.
- Goering, S., Klein, E., Dougherty, D.D., and Widge, A.S., "Staying in the Loop: Relational Agency and Identity in Next-Generation DBS for Psychiatry," *AJOB Neuroscience*, 8 (2017), 59.
- Lázaro-Muñoz, G., Yoshor, D., Beauchamp, M.S., Goodman, W.K., and McGuire, A.L., "Continued Access to Investigational Brain Implants," *Nature Reviews Neuroscience*, 19 (2018), 317.
- The Royal Society, *iHuman: Blurring Lines Between Mind and Machine* (The Royal Society, 2019).
- Chandler, J.A., van der Loos, K., Boehnke, S., Buchman, D.Z., Beaudry, J.S., and Illes J., "Brain Computer Interfaces and Communication Disabilities: Ethical, Legal and Social Aspects of Decoding Speech from the Brain," *Frontiers in Human Neuroscience*, 16 (2022), 1.

GLOSSARY

agonist A chemical that activates a *receptor* to produce a biologic response. Compare: *antagonist*.

allocortex That portion (around 10%) of the *cortex* immediately below the *neocortex*. The allocortex is less complicated structurally than the neocortex and is involved in the evolutionary older sense of smell and in memory. Some anatomists include the *hippocampus* as part of the allocortex.

amygdala The almond-shaped collection of *neurons* embedded within the *rostral* end of the *temporal lobe*. As part of the *limbic system*, it signals the presence of threatening and other salient stimuli and is involved in memory for emotional experiences.

amyloid plaques Extracellular deposits of the amyloid beta protein, mainly in the *gray matter* of the brain. Some plaques occur in the brain as a result of normal aging, but large numbers of plaques (and *tau tangles*) are characteristic features of Alzheimer's disease. How plaques contribute to Alzheimer's cognitive symptoms is uncertain.

analgesic A substance that reduces discomfort associated with painful medical procedures or injury. Compare: *anesthetic*.

anesthetic A substance that eliminates sensitivity to stimulation from medical treatments such as surgery. Local anesthetics eliminate sensitivity by blocking neural signals in one part of the body. General anesthetics, also known as hypnotics, eliminate sensitivity through reversible loss of consciousness. Compare: *analgesic*.

antagonist A chemical substance that decreases the impact of *neurotransmitters* by leading to their faster clearing from the synaptic cleft or by binding with a receptor without activating it, thereby preventing neurotransmitters from binding with it. Compare: *agonist*.

anterior (rostral) A location description meaning toward the front. Your nose is anterior (rostral) to your ears.

anterior cingulate cortex (ACC) The *anterior* portion of the *cingulate cortex*. Wrapping around the *rostral* end of the *corpus callosum*, it contributes to regulation of emotion and the assessment of risks and benefits between prospective actions. It is part of the *risk-reward network*. In experiments asking subjects to impose hypothetical punishment, the ACC is more engaged with the assessment of harm than the assessment of the wrongdoer's intention. Compare *posterior cingulate cortex*.

anterograde amnesia Impairment in forming new event memories after brain damage or disease, preserving long-term memories for events that preceded the damage or disease. Compare: *retrograde amnesia*.

arcuate fasciculus Latin for "curved bundle," and colloquially known as the "language loop," this packet of *axons* connects *Wernicke's area* in the *posterior temporal* and *ventral parietal* *lobes* (for language comprehension) with *Broca's area* in the *frontal lobe* (for language production).

astrocyte A type of glial cell contributing to the *blood-brain barrier*, providing nutrients to nervous tissue, maintaining extracellular ion balance, and repairing or scarring following traumatic injuries.

autonomic The subdivision of the nervous system that controls visceral functions including heart rate, digestion, respiratory rate, salivation, perspiration, pupil size, urination, and sexual arousal; its function is largely unconscious and involuntary.

axial slice See *horizontal slice.*

axon The fibrous extension of a neuron's cell body through which nerve impulses travel to influence muscles, glands, and other neurons.

basal See *ventral.*

basal ganglia A collection of neuron groups deep in the brain that are involved in selecting which movements, thoughts, and emotions are expressed, and in learning to perform tasks automatically. It consists of the putamen and caudate nucleus (also known as the *striatum*), the globus pallidus, the subthalamic nucleus, the nucleus accumbens, and the *substantia nigra.*

base-rate problem A type of logical and psychological fallacy in which people tend to overemphasize the presence of a condition of interest in individual cases and ignore its frequency in the general population.

bilateral On both sides; in neuroscience, a brain structure that appears in each *hemisphere.*

biomarker A measurable indicator of some biological state or condition. Biomarkers are often measured and evaluated using blood, urine, soft tissues, or brain imaging to examine normal or pathological biological processes or pharmacologic responses to a therapeutic intervention.

blood-brain barrier The separation of circulating blood from the extracellular fluid in the central nervous system achieved by the narrowing capillaries interacting with glia. It prevents objects like bacteria and potentially damaging molecules from entering the brain while allowing oxygen, nutrients, hormones, and certain other chemicals to pass.

blood-oxygenation level-dependent signal (BOLD signal) The main measurement currently used for fMRI. It is derived from the ratio of oxygenated to deoxygenated hemoglobin that varies through changes in blood volume, blood flow, and oxygen extraction that are related to neural activity.

BMI See *brain-machine interface.*

BOLD signal See *blood-oxygenation level-dependent signal.*

brainstem The part of the central nervous system at the base of the brain as it becomes the spinal cord, consisting of a collection of various clusters of neurons that are essential for basic functions such as heart beat and respiration; also includes collections of axons traveling between the brain and spinal cord. It includes the medulla, pons, and midbrain.

brain-machine interface (BMI) A direct communication pathway between the brain's electrical activity and an external device, most commonly a computer or robotic limb. BMIs are often directed at researching, mapping, assisting, augmenting, or repairing human cognitive or sensory-motor functions.

Broca's area A cortical area usually in the left *frontal lobe* (of right-handed people) that is essential for the production of speech.

CAT (or CT) See *computed axial tomography.*

caudal See *posterior.*

cell body (soma) The part of the neuron in which proteins and other substances like neurotransmitters and those responsible for the energy supply are synthesized under direction of the genetic material enclosed in the nucleus. Common neurons have many *dendrites* and one *axon* branching off of the cell body.

cellular consolidation One of two types of memory *consolidation* in which molecular processes strengthen synapses in the hippocampus and elsewhere, resulting in stable long-term memories. Cellular consolidation occurs in the hours following the experience that is captured in the memory trace. Compare: *systems consolidation.*

central nervous system (CNS) The brain and spinal cord; distinguished from the peripheral nervous system (PNS), which is comprised of the nerves in the body.

central sulcus The long medial-to-lateral sulcus separating the *frontal* and *parietal lobes.*

cerebellum Literally "small brain," it is a part of the brain tucked beneath the cerebral *hemispheres* on the back of the *brainstem.* It is essential for coordinating complex movements and body posture as well as learning and memory functions.

cerebral cortex See *cortex.*

cerebrum Latin for "brain," it is what most people think of as the brain, namely, the brain proper but without the *cerebellum, brainstem,* or spinal cord.

chronic traumatic encephalopathy (CTE) A neurodegenerative disease linked to repeated trauma to the head. Symptoms include cognitive, behavioral, and emotional impairments. The disease often advances and can result in dementia.

cingulate cortex (cingulate gyrus, cingulate) A *medial* part of the *cortex,* it forms a belt (Latin, *cingula*) wrapping around the *corpus callosum.* Although different parts of the cingulate have functions (*posterior* vs. *anterior cingulate cortex*), this continuous region of cortex is grouped with other structures as part of the *limbic system* and contributes to different forms of emotional regulation, self-control, learning, and memory.

CNS See *central nervous system.*

cognitive control (or executive function) The capacity to adapt neural processing to produce cognition and behavior that is aligned with one's goals and that changes as a function of consequences.

computed axial tomography (CAT, or CT) A neuroimaging technique in which x-rays of the head or body are obtained from many different angles and mathematically combined to yield detailed two- and three-dimensional images.

consolidation In memory research, the theory that some memories, after initial representation in traces of neural activity in the hippocampus, are stabilized into long-term memories. One form is known as *cellular consolidation* and the other as *systems consolidation.*

coronal slice A vertical slice through the head perpendicular to the *anterior* (*rostral*)-*posterior* (*caudal*) axis. Compare: *horizontal slice* and *sagittal slice.*

corpus callosum The large collection of *axons* communicating between the two cerebral *hemispheres,* it has a distinctive bowed appearance in *medial* views of the brain.

cortex From the Latin "tree bark," the layered sheet of *neurons* covering the *cerebrum* and the *cerebellum.* It is folded in the human brain so that a larger sheet can fit in a smaller volume. It is composed mostly (about 90%) of the *neocortex,* which is positioned on the outer surface of the brain and consists of six layers, but also includes the phylogenetically older *allocortex,* which is positioned deeper in the brain.

corticostriatal pathway A circuit between parts of the *cortex* and the *striatum* constituting part of the *risk-reward network.*

cranial nerves Twelve pairs of sensory or motor nerves that emerge from the brain or brainstem to communicate with structures in the head supporting, vision, taste, smell, hearing, facial expressions, and speech.

critical period An interval of limited duration during which experiences are required for brain development. Compare: *sensitive period.*

CT See *computed axial tomography.*

CTE See *chronic traumatic encephalopathy.*

DBS See *deep brain stimulation.*

deep brain stimulation (DBS) Electrical stimulation of structures deep in the brain to treat neurological disorders. The most common is stimulation of parts of the basal ganglia to treat symptoms of Parkinson's disease.

dendrites Protrusions from the *cell body* of a *neuron* resembling the branches of trees that receive input from the *axons* of upstream neurons across *synapses*; dendrites are the input end of a neuron.

diffusion tensor imaging (DTI) A neuroimaging technique that uses *MRI* to map or quantify the integrity of axon fiber pathways in the *central nervous system,* based on the diffusion of water parallel to the neuron fiber pathways.

dopamine A *neurotransmitter* with modulatory actions of excitation and inhibition, depending on its post-synaptic receptor, that contributes to control of body movements, thoughts, and emotions, as well as reward. Dopaminergic neurons are most concentrated in the *substantia nigra* and project to other structures in the basal ganglia and elsewhere in the brain. Drugs of abuse typically act through the dopamine systems of the brain. Parkinson's disease and schizophrenia, among other disorders, involve disorders of dopamine function.

dorsal (superior) A location description meaning toward the top or crown of the head. Your eyes are dorsal (superior) to your mouth.

DTI See *diffusion tensor imaging.*

EEG See *electroencephalography.*

electroencephalography (EEG) A neuroimaging technique that measures on the scalp the magnitude and polarity of weak electric fields generated by neural activity in the brain. It is physically complementary to *magnetoencephalography.*

ERP See *event-related potential.*

episodic memory Memory for events, which includes event features such as times, places, associated emotions, and other contextual knowledge. Compare: *procedural memory* and *semantic memory.*

event-related potential (ERP) A time course of *electroencephalography* or *magnetoencephalography* signal that is generated by averaging across many trials, and is synchronized to the onset of an event, such as a stimulus or a behavioral response. (Sometimes "evoked potential.")

evoked potential See *event-related potential.*

excitable The characteristic of *neurons* whereby they produce rapid and large changes of membrane voltage in response to small inputs.

executive function See *cognitive control.*

fluid intelligence The capacity to reason and solve unique problems.

fluoroscopy An imaging technique, typically used with a contrast agent, that uses x-rays taken in rapid succession to create a movie showing soft tissues moving in real time, such as the heart beating or the tongue moving during speech.

fMRI See *functional magnetic resonance imaging.*

frontal lobe The lobe of the *cerebral cortex* above the eyes, *rostral* to the *parietal lobe.* The *prefrontal* portion contributes to higher-order cognition, including decision-making, self-reflection, goal-directed behavior, and *cognitive control.* The *primary* and *secondary motor cortex* are situated in the most *posterior* portion of the frontal lobe.

functional magnetic resonance imaging (fMRI) A neuroimaging technique that indirectly measures neural activity by detecting changes in the *blood-oxygen-level-dependent* (BOLD) *signal.*

fusiform gyrus A region in the *ventral temporal lobe* important for a host of visual processing functions, including color processing and the ability to sort objects into categories.

glia One of the major types of cells making up the nervous system, outnumbering *neurons* around 10 to 1. Key functions include providing physical sustenance and nutrition to neurons, and other protections through the *blood-brain barrier*, and sheathing *axons* in a coating of *myelin*, which speeds nerve impulse conduction.

gray (grey) matter Dense, organized clusters of *neuron cell bodies* and *glia*.

group-to-individual (G2i) A description of the fundamentally different perspectives of science (including neuroscience), which almost always collects group-level data, and law, which almost always requires findings about individuals.

gyrus (plural: gyri) The rounded folds of the *cerebral cortex* that are separated by *sulci*.

hemispheres The two functionally similar though not identical right and left halves of the brain. There are two hemispheres of the cerebrum, connected by the *corpus callosum*, and two hemispheres of the cerebellum, connected by the vermis.

hemodynamic delay The delay from when *neurons* call for additional blood to meet the metabolic demands associated with increased activity and when the additional blood arrives. This delay is important when analyzing and interpreting results from *fMRI* or other neuroimaging techniques that measure neuronal activity indirectly through changes in oxygenation in the blood.

hippocampus A seahorse-shaped cluster of *neurons* deep in the *medial temporal lobe*. It is usually considered part of the *limbic system* and consists of *allocortex*. It is involved in long-term memory of events, the learning of new facts and concepts, and the representation of space.

homeostasis The self-regulation processes that maintain critical physiological variables such as body temperature, blood pressure, and blood acidity.

horizontal (axial) slice A horizontal slice through the head perpendicular to the *dorsal-ventral* axis. Compare: *coronal slice* and *sagittal slice*.

hypothalamus A set of neuron clusters at the base of the brain that have several functions including regulating blood pressure, body temperature, hunger, thirst, sleep, and circadian cycles. Through connections with the *pituitary gland*, it regulates hormone levels.

inferior See *ventral*.

insula A cortical region buried in the *lateral sulcus* between the *temporal*, *parietal*, and *frontal lobes*. The insula supports *homeostasis*, arousal, pain perception, emotion regulation, sensitivity to disgust (including social disgust at norm violations by others), and decision-making under conditions of uncertainty.

inter-rater reliability In statistics, a measure of the agreement between different persons measuring, rating, or coding the same phenomenon.

language network The principal set of cortical regions and circuits, including *Broca's area*, *Wernicke's area*, and the bundle of axons that connect them, called the *arcuate fasciculus*, associated with the comprehension and production of language. Language also involves two separate pathways between *Wernicke's* and *Broca's* areas and several other cortical areas, including the *ventral* occipital-temporal cortex, ventrolateral *prefrontal cortex*, premotor and motor cortex, plus the *cerebellum*.

lateral A location description meaning toward the side. Your ears are lateral to your nose.

lateral sulcus The major sulcus separating the *temporal lobe* from the *frontal* and *parietal lobes*. Also referred to as Sylvian sulcus.

limbic system The collection of structures encircling the core of the brain involved in emotion, motivation, long-term memory, and olfaction. The limbic system includes the *amygdala*, *hippocampus*, *hypothalamus*, and *thalamus* as well as other structures.

magnetic resonance imaging (MRI) A noninvasive imaging technique providing images of interior body structures. MRI of the brain detects systematic variation of the magnetic properties of atoms in *gray* and *white matter*.

magnetoencephalography (MEG) A noninvasive neuroimaging technique that records the small magnetic fields created by electrical activity in the brain. It is physically complementary to *electroencephalography*.

medial A location description meaning toward the middle. Your nose is medial to your eyes.

medial prefrontal cortex (MPFC) The portion of the prefrontal cortex straddling the brain's midline. The *dorsal* MPFC lies near and is richly connected with the *anterior cingulate cortex* and is associated with several complex functions including self-control, *theory of mind*, and moral decision-making. The *ventral* MPFC lies near and is richly connected with the *orbital frontal cortex* and the *amygdala* and *hippocampus*, among other structures. It is associated with several memory and emotionally salient functions, including regulating emotions in the context of risk assessment (it is part of the *risk-reward network*). When witnessing the violation of a social norm, MPFC contributes to the integration of harm and the norm-violator's intention into a blame signal.

meninges The protective covering of the brain inside the skull consisting of the dura mater, the arachnoid mater, and the pia mater.

mirror neurons *Neurons* that signal when a specific action is produced and when that action is observed being performed by another person. Neuroscientists theorize that mirror neurons are fundamental to the brain circuits enabling *theory of mind*.

myelin A fatty white material derived from *glia* and that wraps around and electrically insulates some *axons*, thereby increasing the speed of nerve impulse conduction.

neocortex The largest (about 90%), evolutionarily newest, and outermost part of the human *cortex*, distinguished from the more primitive *allocortex*.

nerve impulse A brief electrical signal that begins at the *cell body* (soma) and conducts to the tips of an *axon* where it may result in synaptic transmission. Also known as an action potential, or colloquially as a "spike," because of its rapid occurrence.

nerves Bundles of *axons* in the peripheral nervous system. (Bundles of axons in the central nervous system are referred to as tracts.)

neuromodulator A subset of *neurotransmitters* that influence other *neurons* by changing several functions of the effected neurons for a prolonged interval through what neuroscientists call *second messenger systems*. Neuromodulators have diffuse and simultaneous impacts on large groups of neurons.

neuron One of the major types of cells comprising the nervous system. Their excitability and diverse structures with intricate connectivity enable behavior and experience.

neurotransmitter A molecule that conveys the influence of one *neuron* to another. Neurotransmitters are stored within vesicles at the *axon's* end and are released into the *synapse* when an electrical signal passes down the axon. If the neurotransmitter binds to receptors on the dendrites of the receiving neuron, then the receiving neuron will receive a pulse of stimulation, suppression, or modulation.

nociception The process by which *nociceptors* and their pathways in the *central nervous system* create the perception of pain.

nociceptors From the Latin "to hurt," these sensory neurons in the *peripheral nervous system* are responsible for signaling cellular disruption at the body's surface to the central nervous system, which translates the signal into the perception of pain.

norepinephrine A *neuromodulator* associated with arousal and alertness that is made in the brainstem, and a hormone that is made in the adrenal glands. It is chemically related to epinephrine (also known as adrenaline).

occipital lobe The lobe of the *cerebral cortex* at the back of the brain, *caudal* to the *parietal* and *temporal lobes*. It is necessary for visual perception.

orbital frontal cortex (OFC) The area of the *frontal lobe* located behind the forehead and immediately above the eyes and nasal cavity. It contributes to olfaction, emotion, and guiding decisions based on rewards. It is considered part of the *limbic system*.

oxytocin A hormone and *neuromodulator* made primarily in the *hypothalamus* and released by the *pituitary gland*. Its primary function is to facilitate lactation in mammals, but it also promotes pro-social emotional states including pair-bonding, grooming, socialization, trust, cooperation, and empathy.

parietal lobe The lobe of the *cerebral cortex* on the top of the brain, *caudal* to the *frontal lobe* and *dorsal* and *rostral* to the *occipital lobe*. It contributes to the organization of perception and action, and to attention and memory.

PCC See *posterior cingulate cortex*.

peripheral nervous system (PNS) The nerves and somas in the body outside of the brain and spinal cord that connect the central nervous system to the limbs and organs. In contrast to nerve tracts in the central nervous system, nerves in the peripheral nervous system can regenerate.

PET See *positron emission tomography*.

PFC See *prefrontal cortex*.

pituitary gland The endocrine gland located below the *hypothalamus* at the base of the brain. As the "master gland," it secretes hormones that regulate *homeostasis*.

plasticity The capacity of the brain to adapt to injury and experience by changing excitability, altering the shape (structure), or changing the characteristic responses of groups of neurons.

PNS See *peripheral nervous system*.

positron The antimatter counterpart to the electron. Positrons and electrons naturally collide during radioactive decay, releasing two gamma rays (photons) that travel in opposite directions. Gamma rays are used in *PET* and *SPECT* scanning.

positron emission tomography (PET) An imaging technique that produces a two- or three-dimensional image of functional processes (e.g., metabolism) or molecules (e.g., *tau proteins*) in the body by detecting pairs of gamma rays emitted indirectly by a radioactive tracer attached to a biologically active molecule that is injected into the body and conveyed to specific sites in the brain.

posterior (caudal) A location description meaning toward the back. Your ears are posterior (caudal) to your eyes.

posterior cingulate cortex (PCC) The *posterior* portion of the *cingulate cortex*, associated with the regulations of emotion and also part of the *Theory of Mind Network*. In experiments asking participants to impose hypothetical punishment, the PCC is more engaged with the assessment of the wrongdoer's intention than with the assessment of harm. Compare *anterior cingulate cortex*.

pre-occipital notch A landmark in the *cerebral cortex* used to define the boundary of the *occipital lobe* and the *temporal lobe*.

prefrontal cortex (PFC) The portion of the *frontal lobe* located *anterior* to the *secondary* and *primary motor cortex areas*. The PFC contributes to higher order cognition, including working memory, *cognitive control*, and planning.

primary auditory cortex The cortical area in the *superior* part of the *temporal lobe* that initially processes auditory signals.

primary motor cortex A strip of *cerebral cortex* on the precentral gyrus, immediately *anterior* to the *somatosensory cortex* and *posterior* to the *secondary motor cortex*, running from the *medial* surface of the brain down the side toward the ear. The primary motor cortex is necessary for body movement, including fine motor control of the limbs, fingers, and vocal apparatus.

primary visual cortex (striate cortex, V1) The cortical area in the *occipital lobe* that initially processes visual signals.

procedural memory The memory for procedures and processes that underlie motor, visuospatial, or cognitive skills, such as how to play the piano or ride a bike. Compare: *episodic memory* and *semantic memory*.

psychoactive drugs Drugs that affect mental processes of perception, thinking, memory, or feeling.

receptor A cellular protein embedded in a *neuron's* cell membrane that conveys the influence of a *neurotransmitter* when it binds with the receptor. The influence can be an immediate stimulation or suppression for some receptors and neurotransmitters or a prolonged change of state for other receptors and neurotransmitters.

referred pain Pain perceived in the limbs but caused by injury or disease to the spinal cord at levels that innervate the areas of perceived pain.

resting state scans Neuroimaging scans performed on participants while they are not engaged in any goal-directed, purposeful task. Resting state scans are most commonly associated with fMRI, but also can be conducted with EEG and MEG.

retrograde amnesia The loss of memory for events that occurred, or information that was learned, before a neural injury or the beginning of a brain disease.

reverse inference The unwarranted assumption that a given neural signal measured in a particular region of the brain is caused by a given cognitive process because that process is often associated with neural signals in that brain region.

risk-reward network (corticostriatal loop) Circuits between parts of the *cortex* and parts of the *basal ganglia* thought to be critical for the evaluation of the risks and rewards of contemplated action with a crucial contribution of *dopamine* synapses.

rostral See *anterior*.

sagittal slice A vertical slice through the head perpendicular to the medial-lateral axis. Compare: *coronal slice* and *horizontal slice*.

second messenger system A term used by neuroscientists to describe the diverse and prolonged effects of *neuromodulators* that are accomplished by triggering a variety of processes that affect neuronal functions beyond synaptic transmission through chemical cascades.

secondary motor cortex A prefrontal strip on the precentral gyrus, running from the top of the brain down the side toward the ear, immediately anterior to the primary motor cortex. The secondary motor cortex is necessary to plan, organize, and coordinate movements ultimately directed by the primary motor cortex.

selective serotonin reuptake inhibitor (SSRI) A class of drugs, such as Prozac, that increase the concentration of *serotonin* in *synapses* by inhibiting its reuptake into the presynaptic *axon*. They are prescribed to treat depression, anxiety, and some personality disorders.

semantic knowledge Facts, concepts, and other general knowledge about people, places, and things that has been gradually acquired across repeated experiences.

semantic memory Memory for facts, concepts, and general knowledge. Compare: *episodic memory* and *procedural memory*.

sensitive period Intervals of limited duration during which the effects of experience on brain development is particularly strong. Compare: *critical period*.

serotonin A *neurotransmitter* that acts like a *neuromodulator* in some brain areas and is linked to mood, appetite, and sleep. Many antidepressant medications known as *selective serotonin reuptake inhibitors* (SSRI) act by increasing serotonin in the synapses.

single-photon emission computed tomography (SPECT) An imaging technique in which a radioactively labeled molecule is administered to a participant and radioactive decay is measured. Unlike the more expensive PET technique, SPECT detects only the emission of single photons, resulting in less spatial resolution.

sinus A cavity either near the surface of the brain or in the interior of the brain in which deoxygenated blood and other waste products of metabolism are collected to be recycled.

soma See *cell body*.

somatosensory cortex A cortical strip in the *anterior* portion of the *parietal lobe*, running from the top of the brain down the side toward the ear, immediately *posterior* to the *primary motor cortex*. It is involved in our senses of touch, pain, temperature, and limb position.

SPECT See *single-photon emission computed tomography*.

statistical parametric map A statistical technique for examining and depicting differences in brain activity measured during functional neuroimaging experiments. It depicts small volumes (*voxels*) in the brain where differences in measured signals between any two conditions (e.g., a control condition and a task condition) exceed a set statistical threshold.

striate cortex See *primary visual cortex*.

striatum A large part of the basal ganglia, named for the stripes formed by clusters of myelinated axons, which receives inputs from the *cerebral cortex* and midbrain. The *dorsal* striatum is involved with learning habits and acquiring motor skills that, once learned and acquired, can be performed automatically, such as riding a bicycle. The *ventral* striatum is a part of the risk-reward network.

subcortical Referring to brain structures beneath the *cerebral cortex*.

substantia nigra A dark structure located in the midbrain, responsible for the delivery of *dopamine* to the *striatum*. It is identified with the *basal ganglia*. Parkinson's disease is caused by the death of dopamine-producing neurons in the substantia nigra.

sulcus (plural: sulci) A valley or groove formed by the folding of the *cerebral cortex* into gyri.

superior See *dorsal*.

synapse The space between the axonal end of one *neuron* and the dendritic end of a downstream neuron, muscle, or gland into which a *neurotransmitter* is released when an electrical impulse reaches the *axon* terminal.

synaptogenesis The growth of synaptic connections between young neurons during development.

systems consolidation One of two types of memory *consolidation* in which memories initially dependent on the *hippocampus* come to be represented in diffuse regions across the *cortex* and thus no longer depend on the hippocampus. Systems consolidation can occur over days, weeks, months, and even years. Compare: *cellular consolidation*.

tau tangles Fibrous aggregations of a protein called tau, a class of proteins that help maintain axonal structure. Tau proteins can become fibrous and clump together in tangles. The presence of large numbers of tangles, along with *amyloid plaques*, is a characteristic feature of Alzheimer's disease and is associated with impairment in memory function.

tDCS See *transcranial direct current stimulation*.

temporal lobe The lobe of the *cerebral cortex* that is *medial* to the ears, *rostral* to the *occipital lobe* and *ventral* to the *frontal* and *parietal lobes*. It contributes to the recognition and identification of visual and acoustic objects, the representation of *semantic knowledge*, and to the formation and retrieval of *episodic memory*, among other functions.

temporoparietal junction (TPJ) An area at the boundary of the *temporal* and *parietal lobes* that contributes to high-level cognitive functions, including *theory of mind*.

thalamus A bulb-shaped neural mass, about the size of a walnut located in the middle of the brain beneath the cerebral *hemispheres* and above the midbrain. It consists of several subgroups of *neurons* that relay signals to the *cerebral cortex* from sensory inputs and other brain centers.

theory of mind (ToM) The ability of humans (and some other animals) to assess what other individuals are thinking and to adopt the perspective of another individual. It is critical to the legal task of assessing a wrongdoer's state of mind.

Theory of Mind Network The brain network believed to enable *theory of mind,* comprised of the *medial prefrontal cortex,* the right *posterior* superior temporal gyrus, and the right *temporoparietal junction.*

TMS See *transcranial magnetic stimulation.*

ToM See *Theory of Mind.*

TPJ See *temporoparietal junction.*

transcranial direct current stimulation (tDCS) A noninvasive technique for manipulating brain function by delivering weak continuous current to a part of the brain through the scalp.

transcranial magnetic stimulation (TMS) A noninvasive technique for manipulating brain function by delivering strong magnetic pulses close to the surface of the scalp that facilitate or attenuate neural activity in a localized region.

V1 See *primary visual cortex.*

ventral (inferior, basal) A location description meaning toward the bottom. Your mouth is ventral to your nose.

voxel (volumetric pixel) A three-dimensional volume element that is the unit of MRI reconstruction. Depending on how the imaging was performed, voxels can range in size from less than 1 cubic millimeter to up to a few cubic millimeters.

Wernicke's area A region near the *caudal* end of the *temporal lobe,* typically in the left *hemisphere,* around the supramarginal gyrus, that is crucial for speech comprehension.

white matter The *axons* passing between the *cerebral cortex* and other neuron groups; the white appearance is because of the fatty *myelin* sheaths surrounding the axons.

x-ray An electromagnetic wave with high energy and very short wavelength enabling it to pass through many materials opaque to light, making it useful for viewing the internal composition of something, such as the interior of the body.

INDEX

For the benefit of digital users, indexed terms that span two pages (e.g., 52–53) may, on occasion, appear on only one of those pages.